SOUL OF A

CHRISTIAN MAN

a scriptural look at spirituality

SOUL OF A

CHRISTIAN MAN

a scriptural look at spirituality

—— William J. O'Malley ——

ThomasMore®
– An RCL Company –
Allen, Texas

ACKNOWLEDGMENTS
Front cover design by James Ward of Design Block Zero
Inside book design by Kim Layton
Cover photo: Comstock

Send all inquiries to:
Thomas More
An RCL Company
200 East Bethany Drive
Allen, Texas 75002-3804
BOOKSTORES:
    Call Bookworld Companies 888-444-2524 or fax 941-753-9396
PARISHES AND SCHOOLS:
    Thomas More Publishing 800-822-6701 or fax 800-688-8356
INTERNATIONAL:
    Fax Thomas More Publishing 972-264-3719

Visit our website at **www.rclweb.com**

Printed in the United States of America

Library of Congress Catalog Card Number: 99-70054

ISBN 0-88347-431-X

1 2 3 4 5   03 02 01 00 99

This book is for

Michael Connelly

and for

Doug Otis

CONTENTS

INTRODUCTION
MALE SPIRITUALITY

S ince the beginning of human societies, communities have found symbolic ways to celebrate the onset of adulthood in both males and females and to challenge their young to accept, cherish, and begin to understand the entirely new relationship they now have to the community. Due to the mysterious changes puberty has wrought in their bodies, they are no longer children and must begin the always daunting psychological adaptation to adult participation in the community. Physical adulthood happens automatically; psychological adulthood takes effort.

To our impoverishment, our more sophisticated society has let such rituals wither away, except for those few stalwarts who commit themselves to organizations such as the Boy Scouts or Outward Bound. For the rest, adolescence is not an ongoing process, like evolving from infancy to childhood, but a "stage" into which one falls for ten years after puberty—neither child nor adult, but rather in a kind of "moratorium" until college graduation or marriage. Physical adulthood clicks on like a thermostat at puberty; legal adulthood clicks on the day of one's twenty-first birthday. But psychological adulthood does not "click on," and we have few mechanisms with which to help our young activate their human and Christian potential—which need not (and one is tempted to say too seldom does) activate.

In the Roman Catholic Church, confirmation takes place, to the minds of many, too early and with no direct or even indirect reference to the recipient's new role and responsibility in the human and Christian communities *because* of their new physical adulthood. This book, then, is for adult Christian males, a means to share with post-pubescent boys the customs of our "tribe," our legitimate expectations of those now in full adult membership, and to share the adults' own experiences (successes and failures) trying to achieve the challenge of their maleness and of their Christianity in a world which challenges the fulfillment of both. Perhaps it might even invite a more mature Christian male to understand better his own Christianity and his own manhood.

MALE ADULTHOOD AND CHRISTIANITY

All psychologists agree the natural purpose of adolescence is that a former child discover an adult *identity*—an understanding not only of the difference between human beings and animals (moral growth), but also between adult humans and child humans (psychological growth), and between adult males and females (psychosexual growth). In that process, an emergent adult ought to discover at least the rough outlines of who he is: his assets and liabilities, a self he can offer another in the intimacy and partnership of marriage.

The answers to those questions are the foundation for a young person's growing personal conscience and consciousness of a world with far broader horizons than he had known before. Until an individual forms his own personally validated set of rules for legitimate human behavior—interiorizes it—he will be a victim either of the urges of the animal Id (as at a rock concert) or of the strictures of the Superego imposed by parents and teachers (as in Salem, Massachusetts). Most likely, he will be a victim of *both* contradictory voices—in every significant decision.

Therefore, every person recently across the border into the no-man's-land of adolescence ought to begin facing two basic questions: Who am I (an adult, male human, unique individual) and where do I fit into the scheme of things (the web of moral relationships in society)? Unfortunately, the majority of us answer the second question first—often exclusively: Not who am I, but where do I fit in; what attitudes, clothing, behavior (all external to the self) will allow me to be acceptable? Thus, he tries to forge a unique self by becoming like everybody else.

One purpose of this book is to help young (and older) men begin to focus not only on what it means to be an adult human being but what it means to be an adult male Christian.

Christians believe, as all thinking people do, happiness comes from having a good soul, in harmony with all the other souls. But it goes much further. The Kingdom isn't static, living at peace with one's neighbors; It calls for active engagement in their betterment: healing, as Jesus did, even (or especially) the "undeserving." For the World, happiness is security: suburban hedges, insurance policies, police. For the Kingdom, happiness is risk. It is by no means comfortable stasis, but rather the inner peace of the tightrope walker, the helmsman, the rescuer. Although many think comfort is the main product of religion—a placebo—it is not. The gospel parables about hiding one's light and talents preclude that option. As Kazantzakis wrote: Christ is not "Welcome!"; Christ is "Bon voyage!"

To paraphrase Jesus' contrast between the World and the Kingdom: I come not to consume, but to be consumed. Or as John Donne put it, "And I, except You enthrall me, never shall be free, nor ever chaste, except You ravish me." If I want to be useful, then it follows inescapably that, in order to be happy, I have to *be* used.

According to Jesus, happiness comes from surrendering to God and to one's neighbors. "I'm here to bring out the goodness in you, the decency, the healing"—what Gandhi called *satyagraha:* the force of the soul that challenges another soul into coming spiritually alive. Even in a hospital bed, I'm useful: If I'm willing to swallow my pride and offer my need, my very presence says, "Here's a chance for you to reach out and love." The panhandler serves a purpose: "Here I am, an invitation to open your self. But is this an open-hearted gift, or are you going to limit how I can spend it?" The fractious child is a gift: "Do you love me enough to have me hate you for awhile for what you won't let me do?"

Most men I know settle for a *definition* of themselves and their lives rather than a *meaning.* Definition: "I'm a 16-year-old black Catholic student who plays football and works weekends at McDonald's." Definition finds a self as a mixed bag of external roles. Meaning is far less clear-cut, yet far larger, more exhilarating. Tennyson: "I am a part of all that I have met." St. Paul: "I live, no longer I, but Christ lives within me." How does one move inward to the taproot self who weaves all those disparate surfaces into a vivified and vivifying wholeness?

Much confusion arises, I believe, just from the words catechesis uses and has used about the soul, at least in my now rather elongated memory. The age-old use, for instance, of the phrases "to save my soul" or "to lose my soul" seem to indicate my soul is a kind of part of me or a possession, like my hair or my fear of heights or my penchant for vulgarity. To challenge that, I stand in front of a class and say, "You don't see me." ("I told you he was a looney!") But you really don't see me: who I really am. You see only my body—and precious little of that, just the skin that encases all the far more important stuff. You see how I make that body move, hear what comes out of my mouth, notice what consistently elates me or ticks me off, and you make educated guesses about who I really am.

Rather, my soul is myself, all that I am and can be, the essence of who-I-am. I don't *have* a soul; I *am* a soul. I *have* a body, which I trust some day my soul will survive. Although almost nobody really pays much attention to their souls, it is, in fact, everything they are and mean. To neglect the soul is, in effect, to lose it—not in some future hell, but here and now. Failing to attend to one's soul results in a life of meaningless drudgery, a story without a story line.

The first step is to acknowledge one even is a soul, a self below the surface image, and that my soul-self makes the difference between me and an animal. I am not a beast of burden or a rat in a rat race, and because that is a self-evident truth I *refuse* to be treated like one—by my boss, my parents, my pals. Awakening that soul, understanding it, challenging it to grow is what human (as opposed to animal) life is all about! If I haven't begun that process, I haven't begun to live.

Rocks fulfill their divine purpose just by sitting there; the key is in the way God made them. Buttercups and bananas fulfill their divine purpose by taking in food, growing, reproducing, looking beautiful, feeding. Spiders fulfill their divine purpose by spinning webs and retrievers by chasing sticks. If God sends a message to us about what will make us happy, written in the way we are made, different from animals, then the secret of happiness is in the human soul. Animals have bodies and brains, too; only we have the potential which is the soul.

The second step is to realize that soul-self is only a potential; it needn't be activated; it won't evolve without effort. Unlike boulders and bananas and bears, we are the only species free *not* to fulfill our specifically different potential. We are free to act as beasts, vegetables, stepping stones. Or free to challenge that potential into great wholeness, like Thomas More, John XXIII, Terry Anderson. Or free to leave that divine potential fallow, like passively silent drudges, student-zombies, soap opera addicts, managerial robots, mercenaries, hit men. Or free, as far too many good, unhappy people do, just to "get by." As William McNamara says, "Apathy is not the most spectacular form of suicide, just the most common."

The third step is to accept the fact that, yes, a great deal of my personality (as differentiated from—and often opposed to—my character) has been foisted on me by others: defensiveness, aggressiveness, homosexuality, "father wounds"—the whole cornucopia of spiritual, psychic trauma. But from now on, I take responsibility for what happens to what I have, for what I build from the rubble. The two most wasted words are "If only . . . ". Whatever follows them is, *ipso facto,* impossible, and until I free myself of "If only's," I'm quicksanded. As Proverbs 6 says: "How long will you sit there dribbling your time away, moping and wishing your life were otherwise? You are imprisoned in your dreams of might-have-been, self-condemned to circumvent the truth. Make a life from what you have and are. Or die."

This doesn't mean I overlook my faults in smug satis-faction or futile resignation; happiness also hinges on honest confession—which, of course, narcissists avoid as hemophiliacs shun vampires. Nor does it ignore searching for new challenges on higher plateaus. Eros is the life-wish, yearning for wholeness, for impregnation by the Spirit of God, as Our Lady was at the Annunciation. Like any quickening, it can't be hurried, but the fulfilled soul is content, happy, for the moment. Once you know and acknowledge the unique self, once you have an overarching goal that binds all the disparate parts of your life, then the seed has been planted. Get on with it. "Why is fulfillment always in the future?" I am as fulfilled as I can be, for now.

That soul-self—the inner character—is what I make of what's been done to me. I see all the truths of my life and say, "That's all correct and true. Now where do we go from here?"

Perhaps the main reason half of all new marriages today end in divorce is that neither partner has owned a self that can be given in partnership to another. That process of evolving an identity, a self, is the invitation God wrote into the nature of adolescence. Unfortunately, neither schools nor churches seem to find that to be the focused service they ought to offer young people, preferring retaining and returning unusable information, unlittered corridors, attendance at worship. The purpose of education is not merely to train an attractive job candidate. It is to train a good husband and father. This book is meant to help rescue boys we have left treading water.

To find wisdom is to find happiness, and wisdom is serenity in the face of the unchangeable.

Suffering is unchangeable, a given; so is death; so is the resolute refusal of so many potential humans to act humanly. As Holden Caulfield found, once you've wiped out the last "F—— you" graffito from the last wall of a grade school, somebody's going to be scrawling it behind your back. But that doesn't stop you from erasing all the "F—— you" signs you can. Those with a cause—prophets— aren't popular. But they have a sense that, although they won't change much, they—by God—can't be silent anymore. They finally realize there are no innocent bystanders.

Once we make peace with those facts, we can get down to the business of living—abundantly—in what time we have, with the spinach or the spumoni we have on our plates right now. And you don't bother too much with whether there's life after death; you're too busy making sure there's life before death.

THE MALE SOUL

Sam Keen writes in *Fire in the Belly:* "H.L. Mencken once said that the person who coined the term 'near beer' was a very poor judge of distance. I suspect the same error in judgment in the effort to eliminate the distance between men and women." I suspect Keen is right. I know Mencken was.

Before anything else, let me offer a distinction that might help negotiate a thorny field: the distinction between sex and gender—male/female sex on the one side and masculine/feminine gender on the other. Male/female is a matter of bodily fact; the only objective difference between males and females is physical, external or internal genitals—along with whatever psychological differences arise from those physiological differences. Masculine/ feminine (in the Jungian sense) is a matter not of the body but of the soul, the psyche, the self. Unlike the sexual either/or, gender is more/less, a matter of degree, a judgment call.

What Jung meant by "masculine" were all those qualities too long stereotyped to the male, the potential of the left brain: analysis, decisiveness, aggressiveness; by "feminine" he meant qualities too long stereotyped to the female, the potential of the right brain: synthesis, inclusive-ness, intuition. Norman Mailer and Alan Alda are physically virile males, but Mailer is psychologically more aggressive-defensive; Alda is more sensitive-vulnerable. Catherine the Great and Helen Hayes were both physically females; their psychology and "style" were quite different.

The stereotyping has been psychologically corrosive: boys thinking men don't cry and any genuine affection for another male hints at homosexuality; girls believing women are by nature homemakers and any urge to stand up and challenge is a threat to their womanhood. On the contrary, although empathy with "The Elephant Man," even to tears, may be a "feminine" quality in a man, it does not make him *effeminate,* and although rigid analysis may be a "masculine" quality in a woman, it does not make her *macho.* Any unspoken strictures against a boy taking ballet lessons or a girl being a mechanic are strictly subjective, societally induced.

There have been studies of children in their earliest years, before societal customs can have *too* much effect on their psychological predispositions (though with television, a virgin psyche is hard to come by after a child is out of Pampers). Those studies—by Erik Erikson, Janet Lever, and others—seem to show that, by natural desire, boys play outdoors, competitively, and longer than girls, because boys' games are lengthened by arguments over the rules, which the boys seem secretly to enjoy as much as the games themselves. Girls play house, jump rope, hopscotch, and are willing to change the rules—or the game itself— rather than exclude anyone (they like) who is less skilled.

Both boys and girls want to get their own way, but by different means, boys by one-upmanship, girls by persuasion (cf. Samson and Delilah). After about age two, boys continue hitting other children to get their way, but most girls stop, preferring to get their way more by fear of exclusion than by force. Boys judge their place in a group by who gives the orders; girls judge by how alliances shift. Again, how much those preferences are rooted in objective sexual differences and how much is induced by spoken or wordless expectations from parents and from the inescapable TV is difficult to say. But at least for the moment, according to the experts, that is the case: boys are (more) defensive-aggressive, girls are (more) inclusive-adaptable; boys want to compete and win, girls just want to be included in play.

But one objective difference in nurturing makes an important contribution to the male and female psyche, at least since the Industrial Revolution. Since then, most fathers have not worked at home like Pa Walton and Bill Cosby, on the spot, part of both boys' and girls' maturing. Therefore, girls' psyches form with a parent of their own sex, and boys' psyches with a parent of the opposite sex— whether a stay-home mother or day-care personnel or mostly female grade-school teachers. As Deborah Tannen says, a brother and sister grow up "in different cultures."

The boy defines his psyche by *separation* from his mother or mother-substitutes and the girl by *bonding* with them. Boys raise up ego boundaries; girls try to be open and inclusive. That doesn't mean girls develop no sense of a separate self or that boys would find solitary confinement easier than girls. But at least it's a tendency that nurturance generally furthers.

What's more, that separation is now left almost completely to the boy himself, without the assistance more primitive societies gave boys to help them accept their maleness and their position in the society (or Church): rituals wherein the males literally scared boys into adulthood. This causes a kind of silent malaise resulting from what Robert Bly calls a "father wound," since most fathers are no longer available all day at home to help boys with problems their mothers can't resonate with—or feel they can't. Any single-parent mother knows that helplessness.

It is a hunger painfully depicted in *Death of a Salesman:* Biff and Happy, the two soul-dead sons of Willy Loman, who was always on the road. And it is manifest in Willy himself in his hallucinatory, yearning conversations with his dead father-figure brother, Ben. Not only are the sons blighted by that "father distance," but the fathers are impoverished by it as well.

What the new men's movement asks us to consider is that, granting a woman's objective equality in the marketplace, a man isn't a woman and a woman isn't a man, just as a bull isn't a cow and a stallion isn't a mare. When we evolved from our simian cousins, we didn't leave our animal nature behind. Each of us is a psyche, but an *embodied* psyche. Unlike animals, we can make at least some attempt to understand our psychosexual differences and use them to enrich the one life each embodied spirit has.

No embodied spirit is "neuter." A bull is not a cow, but neither is it an ox; a stallion is not a mare, but neither is it a gelding. The women's movement has, mercifully, forced us to see that a father can enrich not only his children but himself by being more "mothering" than his own father would have dared. But the father is not the mother. Witness the incalculable but nonetheless painful incompleteness in a family which has a loving mother but whose father is absent.

Once the aggressive male has been civilized by establishing a healthy relationship with his own "feminine," what Jung called the Anima, he has to go back and re-establish his relationship with his maleness, with what Robert Bly calls his "Wildman." If not, he becomes not merely civilized but domesticated, which is quite different.

Perhaps boys are more aggressive by nature, but they surely are by nurture. As a result of more parenting by someone of the opposite sex, most boys have the need to haggle over rules, duke it out, debate more disputatiously than most girls find comfortable. Perhaps as a result of psychologically distancing themselves from their mothers and establishing ego boundaries, most boys treasure personal freedom, resist being told what to do, being bridled and domesticated.

Ironically, too, the male need to break free, struggle, and take risks also involves vulnerability, a trait formerly too facilely attributed to women. Warlike Achilles had fragile ankles. The male who doesn't realize and bow to that fact is a fool. But the male who does make peace with his own weakness can become a wounded healer. Such vulnerable men are the recovering alcoholics and addicts who can reach out to those now weaker than themselves. Think of the difference, too, between the surgeon who treats his patients like so many biological specimens and the one who cares for them as fellow suffering humans.

Also, when we stopped roaming from one played-out encampment to another, males developed the need to protect, to be responsible, to be accountable. Of course, women have those same needs in order to be fully human, but a male "feels" them in a different, more likely propri-etorial way—surely by nurture. "Patriarch" and "King" have become neuralgic terms in the Church, but males simply can't think of themselves as solely "mothering." There is the need not merely to console but to set things right—which males share with females, surely, but toward which males by nurture feel an irresistible—and frustrating—compulsion.

It is difficult to avoid the conclusion that the official Church acts in regard to both male and female members far less as Holy *Mother* Church than in an almost exclu-sively left-brain, "masculine," analytical, patriarchal way. In contrast, it expects members in the churches—both males and females—to respond in an almost exclusively right-brain, "feminine," submissive way. Even the lower-level all-male clergy are expected to be inoffensive, harmless, acceptable, domesticated, wearing dresses.

Ironically, what men in the pews need from the official Church is *exactly* what a growing number of rightly aggres-sive women have been asking for: empowerment, to share in religious celebration and decision making. Yet, except for deacons, no married man has any more active contri-bution to make than any woman: count the collection, help with the heavier jobs for the parish bazaar, buttonhole fellow parishioners for contributions. Otherwise, they have to defer to the clergy as helplessly as to their plumbers, as if they had nothing to offer but their presence and their pocketbooks.

Whether the male psyche is the way it is from nature or nurture or both, there is little to stir that psyche in Roman Catholic practice today. Nor is it only the liturgy, with its Hallmark hymns and passive "participation," which impov-erishes both male and female spirits. The picture of Jesus we get from even the best biblical movies is one I call "Jesus, the Warm Fuzzy" and which Old Testament scholar Patrick Arnold calls "the Bearded Lady." The apostles and saints seem just as neutered, like the "safe" pictures of St. Joseph, old and no longer a sexual threat.

The very challenge that made the Church important to young men in periods when it was genuinely apostolic now seems irrelevant: the "masculine" solidity of the word "Kingdom" (for both males and females) has been toned down to the less threatening—and less stirring—"Realm." Not much adventure there, not a Kingdom to be won but a Realm already cozily established. The God for whom we struggle is no longer "King" but "Sovereign"; not "Father" but a neuter "Parent." The Ignatian meditations on the Kingdom and the Two Standards are now almost heretical to the tenets of Catholic political correctness.

The Christian women's movement makes a strong and valid criticism of the centuries-old patriarchalism and male dominance not only in Church governance but in liturgical language, and we must do all we can to rectify that dismissive injustice. But in righting the balance, we must remember that males have souls, too, and that the male psyche (if not by nature, at least by nurture) is significantly different from a female's. What's more, we must acknowledge that, down through the centuries, religion has always been deemed by many males to be "womanish."

Granted God is not male, my experience of God shows that if the Creator is a mother, she's one tough cookie. Granted also God is nurturing, supporting, enfolding and rapturously creative, God has also dealt me some pretty bitter blows over the years and has rarely paused to give me reasons for them. And it's very difficult to take a walk and bawl hell out of an Old Friend of 65 years who seems to have betrayed my trust (again)—and forgive God—when God has suddenly become a neutered "Parent."

If there is anything true of a fully actuated male, it is an aversion to homogenization. The male soul thrives on challenge, the heroic, the wild, the individuated—qualities not expected in Catholic males, in the pew or in the pulpit. At work, a man is expected to be a stallion; at Mass, to metamorphose into a gelding. That temporary neutering is not possible. What Catholic males need to regain is our sense of pilgrimage, of the bloodless crusade: the Grail Quest.

WHAT CAN WE DO?

Positively, what can Catholic ministry—that is, healing—do to save the Christian male's soul, not from some future hell but from atrophy here and now? It is unlikely any of us can affect the official Church's attitudes regarding unordained males, but what can we do at the level of the schools and parishes to offer genuine life to the male-embodied soul?

The very first step is to recognize and accept that we have a real problem. Unless we admit we have a crisis, we will go on congratulating ourselves for doing a good—or at least adequate—job "saving souls." We must admit, on the one hand, that most males are turned off by "churchy stuff," but on the other hand that most males are still hungry spirits.

Most males are not roused by the Catholic experience. Next Sunday, count heads to see the proportion of women to men at Mass; quite likely it will be three to one, sometimes even five to one. The official structure of the Church is unbendingly "masculine," but the soul-life of the Church is overly "feminized" and unappealing (and certainly unstirring) for the male soul, no matter what the source of that resistance.

It is unarguably true that the difference between Christianity and nearly every other Western world religion is that it *was* open to the civilizing, humanizing, and divinizing values of the "feminine," surely more "feminine" than the Jewish or later Islamic patriarchies. The gifts which St. Paul says come from the Holy Spirit are: love, peace, patience, kindness, goodness, fidelity, gentleness and self-control. All "feminine."

But no one can argue that Jesus or Paul went about their task of spreading that liberating "feminine" message in a "feminine" way. As Pat Arnold writes, "Masculinity is *assumed* in early Christianity and shoots through the whole New Testament like an electric charge: Jesus' bold confrontations with the Pharisees, Peter's courageous leadership of the new sect, Paul's aggressive missionary strategy, and so on. Most of the first generation was martyred for its beliefs—hardly a mark of the meek and mild!" (And those resilient souls were both males and females.) The Catholic Counter-Reformation and the new Jesuit spirituality rang with military metaphors that appealed not only to the "masculine" in males but also to the fully realized "masculine" in the healthy female soul. After all, both Joan of Arc and Dorothy Day were females.

Catholic males are indebted to the women's movement for forcing them to encounter their own "feminine." But they have now been stranded in a nearly exclusively "feminine" spirituality which turns them off: butterflies and balloons. (I was criticized the other day for calling a boy "manly.") Such a lopsided approach to the soul is erosive not only to male spirituality but to female spirituality as well!

On the other hand, Catholic males do have "a God-sized void" that is left hungry, and the soul settles for The Great Numbness, the inability to feel joy or meaning or grief or *anything*. Bland, boring, homogenized. There is no "rush" to being a male Christian today, no sense of greatness; so, many of our young and not so young settle for beer and football, *machismo* and horseplay, drugs and casual sex: junk food for the soul.

The woundedness of the male soul is manifest in statistics that show men can expect eight fewer years of life than women, commit suicide three times as often, be more likely victims of alcohol and drugs, and suffer disproportionately more fatal illnesses. Men are the most frequent perpetrators—and victims—of assault and murder and outnumber women in prisons nine to one.

Sam Keen makes the case that, just as the cathedral was the sacred center of a medieval city, now banks and commercial buildings are the center of the modern city. "The Dow," Friederich Franck writes, "has replaced the Tao." But corporations, universities, and government are all suffering from burnout, often in men who have never truly been on fire! "Stress cannot be dealt with by psychological tricks," Keen says, "because for the most part it is a philosophical rather than a physiological problem, a matter of the wrong worldview." It is not a sickness of the mind but of the spirit. The same could be said for disspirited sex. "We are able to lose ourselves in loving sexuality only to the degree that we have found the self elsewhere. It takes a very secure person to surrender to another in love."

What's more, the soulless marketplace—"the jungle"—is infectious. It is wrenchingly difficult for a man to keep his guard up all day and then switch gears into the loving father, the sensitive husband, the compassionate friend. If we could first convince men of the absolute need of at least a half-hour a week to meditate and pray, and then teach them methods of centering, we might give men not only a sense of personal meaning and hope but vigor again.

Perhaps men do not realize that the malaise—what Thoreau called "quiet desperation"—is a hunger of the starved spirit, that they truly *need* an active relationship with God and their own souls, even though they don't yet *want* one. But that "soullessness" is evident not only in the grinding routine of many adult males but in a great many becoming-adult males as well: the blahs, the spiritlessness of senioritis, aversion to commitment or any incursions on freedom, often trying to prove to everybody that they even have a self and are "here" through graffiti and boom boxes blasting out territorial claims, and at worst "wilding" sprees and random shootings of strangers.

There's a hunger there all right, but most males don't find that hunger appeased in the Catholic Church. Certainly, dramatically fewer males want to dedicate their lives to "her."

Yet consider the entire male-fixated Arab world coming to a halt five times daily in order to manifest its belief in the power and peace of Allah, Hindu and Buddhist monks abounding all over Asia, Jewish men pressing their palms and foreheads to the Western Wall in Jerusalem. Perhaps other world religions do boast an overly "masculinized" religiosity. But modern Christian spirituality seems to eschew it altogether, and the "God-sized hunger" other males in the world find no hesitation in satisfying. That hunger rumbles in the male Catholic soul, unsatisfied and often not even understood as the restlessness that can be satisfied only by God. "Don't worry. I can handle it myself."

Christianity is a religion of love, but love is ordinarily limited in our minds to compassion, healing, forgiveness. Yet love is also active, dynamic, aggressive, even "tough." The Holy Spirit is a spirit of fire! And every mystic who ever suffered the Spirit's love has been aware of the burning. Love is not always gentle; it is sometimes fierce, challenging, relentless. That is the kind of Christian love men need far more of.

HOW TO USE THIS BOOK

There are many varied ways to benefit from reading this book: 1) for your own spiritual growth; 2) as you make your way along the spiritual journey with others; 3) for young men in the "beginning" stages—either in high school or college. An appendix has been crafted to help foster adult discussion groups. The hope and expectation is that adult men will be encouraged to pray and share experiences with each other, both in informal and formal settings. Men of all ages who are looking for a way to enhance their spirituality will find the biblical role models especially helpful as they make their own way along the spiritual path.

AN INITIATION RETREAT

Soul of a Christian Man will also be helpful in starting younger adult males on their journey into manhood. One way to use this book might be to give a younger adult male a copy, ask him to read through it, subsection by subsection, and write down questions that pop into his mind so he can thrash it out with an adult male he trusts who has also read it.

A parish or school which acknowledged the need for a distinctively male soul-life could organize a team of fathers who would go away for a weekend with boys who have undergone puberty, to explain not only their new function in the human family but also in the Church. Jesus was not a lecturer; he taught with stories. Let each session, then, begin with a story which embodies some aspect of the uniquely male psyche: the need to develop the "feminine" Anima, to return then to what Robert Bly calls the Wildman, to be both warrior and wounded healer, to be a prophet who stands up confidently, relying not merely on his own self-esteem but on The One Who Calls and Sends.

After the story, instead of "explaining" what the story is trying to tell about male Christian adulthood, probe the story with the boys—in small groups if possible—to find out what *they* find in the story. Then let the men and boys go off in pairs or, if the group is large, two or three boys with one adult. Let each man tell the boys his own story: his struggles with his sexuality, his need to pray, his concerns about his family, his expectations of himself as a Christian male. The final chapter offers questions boys could be given to ask the men about the focus of each story.

Finally, let the weekend conclude with a eucharistic meal during which there is a ceremony of initiation as Christian adults with some kind of token of induction that the boys would find meaningful and memorable. Not boys anymore. Young men.

Perhaps, too, once every six months, there could be one Sunday Mass just for the older and younger men who have made such retreats, so that they could continue to explore the one God and their own uniquely embodied male souls.

If the Church would pursue such strategies actively to elicit those qualities in males, there would be fewer men and boys holding up the rear wall of the church—or home watching Charles Osgood. Surely it would profit not only the boys but the adult men, who would not only understand but experience that they *are* integral elements in the soul-life of the Church. And they would experience their own souls as growing, in an atmosphere where no one need apologize for being part of a Kingdom focused on a Grail they discovered where it first began, on a eucharistic table at which men were not embarrassed or uneasy to sit. A meal where wounded warriors were welcome.

1 THE HERO

In this selection from John Updike's Rabbit Run, *Harry "Rabbit" Angstrom is twenty-six, 6'3," and lives and works in Mt. Judge, a grungy town outside the fifth-largest city in Pennsylvania. Eight years ago Rabbit had been the best basketball player in his high school and was famous through the county. Now he demonstrates Magi-Peel Vegetable Peelers in five-and-dime stores. His wife has stopped being pretty; now she is pregnant again and alcoholic. It's Friday night. And on his way to pick up his son, whom his wife has dumped at his mother's, Rabbit simply takes off in his old car.*

Route 23 works west through little tame country towns, Coventryville, Elverson, Morgantown. Rabbit likes these. Square high farmhouses nuzzle the road. Soft chalk sides. In one town a tavern blazes and he stops at a hardware store opposite with two gasoline pumps outside . . .

"Couldya fill it up with regular?"

The man starts to pump it in and Rabbit gets out of the car and goes around to the back and asks, "How far am I from Brewer?"

The farmer looks up with a look of curt distrust from listening to the gas gurgle. He lifts a finger. "Back up and take that road and it's 16 miles to the bridge."

Sixteen. He has driven 40 miles to get 16 miles away.

But it was far enough, this was another world. It smells differently, smells older, of nooks and pockets in the ground that nobody's stirred yet. "Suppose I go straight?"

"That'll take you to Churchtown."

"What's after Churchtown?"

"New Holland. Lancaster."

"Do you have any maps?"

"Son, where do you want to go?"

"I don't know exactly."

"Where are you headed?" The man is patient. His face at the same time seems fatherly and crafty and stupid . . .

"Check the oil?" the man asks after hanging up the hose on the side of the rusty pump, one of the old style, with the painted bubble head.

"No. Wait. Yeah. You better had. Thanks." Simmer down. All he'd done was ask for a map. Damn dirtdigger so stingy, what was suspicious about that? . . .

The man lets the hood slam down and smiles over at Harry. "That's $3.90 on the gas, young fella:" the words are pronounced in that same cautious, crippled way.

Rabbit puts four ones in his hand. . . The farmer disappears into the hardware store; maybe he's phoning the state cops. He acts like he knows something, but how could he? . . . Switching off the lights in the hardware stores as he comes, the farmer comes back with the dime and the man pushes it in with his broad thumb and says, "Looked around inside and the only road map is New York State. You don't want to go that way, do you now?"

"No," Rabbit answers, and walks to his car door. He feels through the hairs on the back of his neck the man following him. He gets into the car and slams the door and the farmer is right there, the meat of his face hung in the open door window. He bends down and nearly sticks his face in. His cracked thin lips with a scar tilting toward his nose move thoughtfully. He's wearing glasses, a scholar. "The only way to get somewhere, you know, is to figure out where you're going before you go there."

THE HERO AS A MAP

Every year for 32 years I've put the word "SUCCESS" on the board at the high school where I teach and gone up and down the rows asking each young man what the content of that word was for him as an individual. In all those years, three and four times each year, the response has been absolutely invariable. In the first place, the answers are always in near whispers, as if the speaker didn't really want to be heard. In the second place, only one or two in each class had the bravado to say, "Money!"—as if money hadn't been an absolute essential in the back of all the other students' minds. And in the third place, except for those who mentioned money, the content of "success" was sublimely vague: "To, uh, achieve your goals . . . To be, uh, happy . . . To, uh, have a good life." But what do those words *mean*? Never once in 3,000-plus replies has anyone said, "To be a good father and husband . . . To be a research biologist . . . To do something meaningful for the homeless."

The trouble is you can't achieve a vague goal. "Where ya goin'?" "Oh . . . *some*where, that's for sure. Some . . . where." Like Rabbit, you can't shop for a map till you have at least a general idea where you want to go. College seniors I talk with evenings in the dorm often tell me, in March of their final year, that they're not sure "yet" what they're going to do. But not to decide is to decide, to drop the decision into the hands of fate is to end up forced to take whatever job they can get, even if they don't like it, because on graduation day welfare stops.

No one can blame a high school student for not having a tightly focused goal: doctor, lawyer, businessman—though it's wise even at that early stage to start narrowing down the possibilities, at least to the point of crossing out all those you *don't* want, which at least makes the number of choices less intimidating. But no matter what specific career an adolescent boy chooses, he certainly is being invited to become an adult male. What's more, although everyone agrees schooling is to prepare an attractive job candidate, not many accept the fact that one's adolescent years are also an invitation to prepare a good husband and father.

Note: It's an *invitation*, not a command that can't be refused nor an inevitable outcome that will just fall into place if you wait long enough. We all know men physically grown up but neither adult nor manly: the whiners, the grudge-bearers, the braggarts, the tyrants, the terminal adolescents like Sam Malone and his bar cronies. They're men without either goals or maps who drift along, victims of whatever happens next.

Before the Industrial Revolution, boys had their fathers working at home, taking as much part in their maturing as their mothers. Since then, however, most fathers work a considerable distance away, and the boys have to find their adult selves more with their mothers, persons of the opposite sex, rather than with their fathers. Today, a great many boys don't have even that, since their mothers also work away from home, and of those boys born in the year 2000, about half will grow up in a single-parent home or with a male figure who is not their natural father.

What's more, skepticism set in since the Kennedy and King assassinations, Vietnam, Watergate, Iran-Contra, the hostages, *The National Enquirer.* It's become very "uncool" to have heroes, because sooner or later heroes are going to let you down: get caught using steroids, cheat on their wives, contract AIDS.

More and more when I ask seniors their heroes, nearly half say, "I don't think I have any heroes." Some who do mention names give pretty weird combinations, like

Mother Teresa *and* Donald Trump. The sad part is that they honestly believe they can model their lives on both. The other heroes are almost all rock stars and athletes, whom they admit they admire not because they've done anything of substance but because they've had the smarts to parlay modest talents into million-dollar paychecks and live enviably in the fast lane. A recent Almanac annual poll of youngsters in malls asking for their heroes said the hero of that year was Tom Cruise; the year before it was Eddie Murphy—slick, uncommitted, flashy, sexy, but no genuine substance.

Movies like *Rambo* and *Conan the Barbarian* also give a false, shallow idea of what it's like to be an adult male. A *real* man loves football, beats hell out of anyone who gets in his way, never weeps, "scores" as often as possible, keeps his guard up and his feelings hidden, suppresses compassion, fear, and especially guilt. Magazines like *Playboy* and its host of imitators offer enough peekaboo titillation to supply a grown-up's adolescent masturbatory fantasies for a lifetime. Even the ads offer the same shallow message: beer, booze, sports clothes and equipment, stereos, sports cars, and cigarettes—all the things that make a real man, right? A real father and husband?

That's a greater loss than at first one might realize. For thousands of years young men had heroes like Achilles, Arthur, The Deerslayer, Lindbergh, Tom Dooley, Martin Luther King to show them what a real man looks like, what makes him different from a grown-up boy: self-confidence, pluck, idealism, responsibility, curiosity, the wits to rise out of sticky situations, the courage to challenge and change. They served as a map to becoming the man a wife and children could look for as a husband and father, what a community could look for in an adult male.

The women's movement has made major and welcome inroads on the Caveman-Viking-Rambo false image. They have been working on civilizing boys and men since the days of ancient Greece when Aristophanes wrote "Lysistrata," and they've finally begun to succeed. Many husbands now do chores around the house even their own fathers would never have thought of doing: cleaning, cooking, diapering. Men have begun unashamedly to contact the "feminine" side of themselves, what psychologist Carl Jung calls the "Anima." Half the girls in my dorm have on their walls a picture called *"L'Enfant,"* a chesty young guy, shirtless, staring in awe at his baby on his knees who's staring back in awe at him. That's the kind of man they want: a hunk with a heart.

But it's not enough, because though a father needs to learn a great deal about fathering from the mother, the father is *not* the mother.

A great many men who have been liberated from the tyranny of the Wildman, "feminized," remain there: comfort-loving, surviving without living, able to nurture but balking at commitment, uncomfortable standing up against the crapstorm. In a word, "domesticated." Many of them get into their 40s and suffer burnout—without ever having been on fire!

A good many of the readers of this book are probably young men with unfocused, vague, "generic" goals. They have a half-formed idea of what they want to be "when they grow up," and it's quite often "the usual": decent job, home in the suburbs, with a trustworthy (and desolatingly sexy) wife, 1.5 kids, and maybe a pool in the yard, a membership in a club, a home at a lake. But is that all there is? You only go around once. Is that all you want to accomplish: to survive for 70 years and disappear? Or do you want to make a difference?

That's what this book is for: to invite men to become *adult* males in their spirituality rather than just *grown-up* males. But it is, again, an invitation, not a command or a sure thing. It takes effort, which you're free to refuse. But freedom is a tricky reality. It's like money in your pocket, comforting to have, but it doesn't activate until you actually *spend* it on something you genuinely want. So, too, with freedom. You're free to be anything your talent and luck allow you to be—*but* only once you commit yourself, freely, to one goal, and by that fact surrender all others. Not to decide *is* to decide. Not to choose to be *somebody* is automatically to choose to be *nobody*.

Richard Wilbur, author of *Ceremony and Other Poems*, has a poem that captures it:

> *I read how Quixote in his random ride*
> *Came to a crossing once, and lest he lose*
> *The purity of chance, would not decide*
> *Whither to fare, but wished his horse to choose,*
> *For glory lay wherever he might turn.*
> *His head was light with pride, his horse's shoes*
> *Were heavy, and he headed for the barn.* *
> *Ceremony and Other Poems, NY: Harcourt Brace, 1950

THE ARCHETYPES

Carl Jung discovered what he called "archetypes" in all the major folk stories of all the cultures of the world—a kind of stripped-down model of the major factors that differentiate between a hero and a nobody, between a knight and a pawn.

A synonym for "archetype" is "prototype," the original according to which all later models are patterned. For our purposes here, they are the qualities which societies throughout the centuries have found make an honorable and fulfilled adult male. Those ideal qualities have been embodied in stories of heroes who possessed them in an admirable way: Odysseus, Aeneas, Beowulf, King Arthur, Robin Hood, Geronimo, Jackie Robinson, and the stories were sung and read to young boys to instill in them a vision of the kind of men the community expected them at least to try to become. The Bible is filled with the same kinds of stories, as we will see.

But each archetype also has a "Shadow" side, the animal energy which, on the one hand, gives vibrant life and power to that male quality but which, on the other hand, can run amok if it is unchecked by its opposite qualities. The Patriarch in a man, for instance, gives him the force and confidence to take charge, yet if it is unchecked by genuine care and affection it can run wild into tyranny. In order to be a profitable member of the community, a man must tame his tigerish spirits contained in the Shadow, yet if he checks them *too* much, he becomes no more than a domesticated pussycat. As Jung said, "the animal in us becomes more beastlike" when it is completely suppressed. One has only to consider the cruel treatment of witches in simon-pure Salem or the serial killers whose neighbors describe them as quiet, timid young men.

We will consider some of those archetypes here, triggering ideas about what makes a noteworthy man by studying first brief lives of several Old Testament heroes and Jesus. Most likely at the end of this you won't have a detailed map of where your life as a male is headed, but you'll quite probably have a far less fuzzy and "generic" sense of direction.

Below is a general scheme of the book, each of the prophets, what archetype(s) he embodies, and the values that archetype proposes which most men are too busy or too lazy—or too frightened—to develop in themselves.

But any virtue, unchecked by its opposite, runs amok into a vice. Love, unchecked by common sense, goes crazy into sentimentality or "smotherlove;" humility, unchecked by genuine self-esteem, turns a man into a doormat. Just so, Jung says each of the archetypes, unchecked by its opposite, runs wild to the "Shadow" side. It takes over when the major assets of the type aren't *balanced* by their opposites. In the final column (in a very schematic way here at the outset) is the element in a man's character which will keep that quality, once stimulated, from taking over and running wild.

	Archetype	Shadow	Balance
ABRAHAM			
Pilgrim	*Challenge to change*	*Aimless wandering*	*Purposeful resolve*
Patriarch	*Big-hearted decisiveness*	*Tyranny*	*Fatherlove*
MOSES			
Warrior	*Courageous confidence*	*Self-serving; bullying*	*A code of honor*
Magician	*Intuitive inventiveness*	*Cunning egotism*	*Humility*
JONATHAN			
Friend	*Loyalty*	*Dependency*	*Self-reliance*
SOLOMON			
King	*Responsibility for others*	*Tyranny*	*Concern for others*
ELIJAH			
Wildman	*Freedom and adaptability*	*"Wilding"*	*Service*
Healer	*Aggressive challenge of "illness"*	*Using spiritual power to harm*	*Emotional control*
JEREMIAH			
Prophet	*Devotion to the truth*	*Self-pity; burnout*	*Confidence in God*
JONAH			
Trickster	*Exuberant fun*	*Terminal adolescence*	*Meditation; a schedule*
JESUS			
The Whole Man	*Fulfillment of all the archetypes*		

All those archetypes—and their shadows—are sleeping within your soul, but they won't waken on their own, as puberty did, nor will anyone force you to swallow them piece by piece, like trigonometry. The choice and the effort are all your own. There are only two alternatives: to be somebody, or to be nobody.

And not to decide is to decide.

Glory? Or the barn?

For further discussion see the appendix,
pages 175–177.

2 ABRAHAM:
Pilgrim / Patriarch

Once upon a time north of Canaan, there lived this man and woman named Abram and Sarai, very, very old, very, very rich, and barren as a pair of bricks. But with plenty of sheep, goats, slaves, and silver, it was not the worst life in the world.

But the Lord God has an aversion to comfortable self-satisfaction. Just when you've got your life settled and serene, he shows up and whistles, "Up an' at 'em, Abram! We're hitting the road! I've got plans! I'm going to give you a new land and a host of descendants. Let's go!" And without so much as goodbye, the Lord God walks away, trailing light behind him.

Dutiful believer, Abram suppressed the urge to remind the Lord God that Sarai was a bit long in the tooth to conceive a child, but instead he collapsed his tents and gathered his wife, his nephew Lot, his slaves and cattle and all his possessions, said goodbye to his puzzled lifelong neighbors, and set off south for the land of Canaan and the life of a pilgrim.

Now the Canaanites were none too tickled to see this horde of hairy barbarians and a whole honking, hooting, howling horde of animals surge into their comfortable country, but Abram sat with the chieftains and parleyed for grazing land, and water holes: the head of his clan.

The hill grass was good, but water holes few, so Abram's herdsmen and his nephew Lot's herdsmen constantly squabbled. So the two met, and Abram said, "Choose whatever area you want," so Lot camped near the wicked city of Sodom in the Jordan valley, and Abram stayed in the hill country. And everything looked like peace was here to stay. They thought.

No sooner had the two clans settled when four chieftains from the north raided Sodom and marched off with everything that wasn't broken—including Lot, his family, and cattle, and led them all toward slavery in the north. One man escaped to bring the news to Abram. As father-chief, Abram had no choice but to rescue his family, so he rounded up his men and set off in hot pursuit. One night, stealthily, Abram's men crept into the encampment, overcame the guards, and rescued Lot and his goods. And everyone went home to normality. If there is such a thing.

And the Lord God stopped around occasionally, blazing with light, to chat with Abram about the great plans. But after ten years of promises, Abram's patience wore a bit thin. "Lord God," he said, "where are these descendants?" Instead of answering, the Lord led Abram out and pointed to the dark sky spangled with stars. "Try to count them," he said. "You will have that many descendants." So Abram trusted, and the Lord God smiled.

But Sarai was more inclined to take matters into her own hands. "Your God!" she snapped. "Ten years! No children! My Egyptian slave, Hagar. Take her. If she has a child, it will be my child." So Abram did, and Hagar became pregnant.

No sooner was Hagar pregnant than she began getting snippy, playing the grand lady to the servants. "*I'm* carrying the father-chief's child, *amn't* I?" she sneered. "Not dried-up Sarai."

Well, patience wasn't one of Sarai's noticeable virtues, so she grabbed Abram by the beard: "That snip despises me! *Do* something!" But Abram held up his hands: "All right! She's your slave! Do what you want." So Sarai did precisely that, treating the girl so cruelly Hagar fled into the hills toward Egypt.

But as the exhausted pregnant girl trudged wretchedly along, she encountered the shining Lord God. "Where are you going, child?" the Lord God asked. "Away from my cruel mistress," she whimpered. "There, there," the Lord God said. "Go back and serve her. I promise: The child you carry will be the father of uncountable descendants, a separate people. He will be Ishmael, 'God hears,' because I heard your weeping." So Hagar returned, and within a few months she bore Abram his firstborn, Ishmael.

Thirteen more long years dragged by, and the Lord God stopped again at Abram's tent. "I will make mutual covenant with you. Your name will now be Abraham, 'Father of Multitudes.' On your side, circumcise every male in your family and every new male at the age of eight days." When Abram sort of winced at that, the Lord said, "Whoever rejects circumcision rejects our covenant. Sarai will be called Sarah, 'Mother of Nations.'"

Despite himself, Abraham giggled. "Lord," he said, "No offense, but Sarai hasn't had her periods in many years. Let Ishmael inherit. You told Hagar he would have many descendants."

"Ishmael was Sarah's idea, not mine," the Lord smiled. "I have other plans for Ishmael. Father of a great Arab nation. But I will keep special covenant with Sarah's son, whom you will call Isaac, 'He giggles.'" The Lord God, smirking, walked away. Dutifully, that very day Abraham was circumcised with all males in his household. And he waited. And waited.

One day Abraham sat at his tent flap and saw three shining presences emerge from the haze. He pressed his face into the dirt. "Excellencies, you honor my home." And the three sat.

The Leader said, "Nine months from now, I will be back, and your wife will be holding her son." But just inside the tent, Sarah was eavesdropping, and she giggled. "Why did Sarah giggle?" the Visitor asked. "Is anything too hard for the Lord God?" Red-faced, Sarah stumbled from the tent. "I . . . I did *not* giggle," she said. "Yes," the Visitor grinned. "You giggled."

True to the Lord's word, nine months later, Sarah delivered a son: Isaac, "He giggles." And the boy grew strong, and each time Abraham looked at the child, his heart quickened.

But his joy was not untroubled. Two sons. Two mothers. Who would inherit? The firstborn of the slave, or the younger of the true wife? That question was never far from the minds—and loud lips—of Sarah and Hagar, and Abraham remembered the time he was silently sonless. Then one day, Sarah saw Ishmael tormenting Isaac and rushed to her husband. "I want that slave and her brat gone! Now!" Abraham fretted; Ishmael was his son, too. But the Lord God had told him there were other plans for him. So next morning, Abraham watched woefully as Hagar and her gangly boy trudged into the wilderness.

Later he heard with sadness Ishmael had become a great hunter, wandering alone like a wild ass, set against everyone and everyone against him, tough-souled and bitter.

Then one day when Isaac was in his teens, and Abraham was savoring his old age, he heard a voice. "Abraham?" He knew it was The Great Surpriser, and he stammered, "Yes, Lord God." And the Lord God said, "Take Isaac. Go to the land of Moriah. There on a mountain I will show you, offer him as a sacrifice to me."

Abraham's heart stood still; his stomach turned to ice. How many years had he waited? But he rose and cut the wood, put it on a donkey, and called for Isaac, the son of the promises.

For three days, Abraham trudged the hills toward Moriah, the bright-eyed boy skipping beside him, puzzled at the heaviness in his old father. On the third day, Abraham saw a grove, and he knew he had reached the place of destiny. So he loaded Isaac's arms with the wood and began to climb toward the grove, the pot of hot coals swinging at his side.

"Father?" Isaac asked. "We have coals and wood; where is the lamb?" Abraham choked back his tears. "The Lord God will provide, my son." And the two walked on together.

At the center of the grove, Abraham built a rough altar of stones and arranged the kindling and logs. Then he turned to Isaac, wide-eyed, trembling, unable to move as his father came toward him with the leather straps. Tears streaming down his wrinkled face, Abraham bound the whimpering boy with the straps and lifted him onto the sacrificial pyre. He pulled his dagger and raised it high over the throat of all he loved best.

"Abraham!" came the voice of God.

"Yes," Abraham choked. "Here I am."

"Don't hurt the boy. Enough. Now I know there is no one worthier of my trust than you, because you have not kept back even this child if I asked. Look behind you."

Abraham looked round and saw a ram, the iron curls of its horns caught in a thicket. He wrestled it free and brought it to the altar and sacrificed it instead of his son. And Abraham called that place "God Provides."

Male Archetypes in ABRAHAM

	Archetype	Shadow	Balance
Pilgrim	Challenge to change	Aimless wandering	Purposeful resolve
Patriarch	Big-hearted decisiveness	Tyranny	Fatherlove

THE PILGRIM

Abraham had a compass: the voice of the Lord God. He was not merely a directionless wanderer, but a pilgrim on his way to a destination he did not know, but which he trusted the Lord God knew. He was unafraid of challenge and change, confident not only in his own abilities but in the One who calls and sends.

From nowhere comes this unnerving challenge: "Come out on the road with me!" Think of the cost to Abram. He'd poured his life into the land; he cared for his neighbors, knew every well and wadi within a hundred miles of his encampment. He was wealthy, but in the great world, a nobody. Yet something in his soul was *ready* when the lightning struck: the Inner Pilgrim.

Sigmund Freud enunciated the difference between true human pleasure (which first looks appalling) and false human pleasure (which first looks appealing). True pleasure he called *Eros*, the life wish, which rises to challenge, even at the risk of losing something valuable; false pleasure he called *Thanatos*, the death wish, which yearns to be unbothered, even at the risk of stagnation.

Eros, the life wish, pushes us toward a larger life—birth, growth, independence from parents, parenthood—even at the cost of suffering: losing something good in the hope of something better. All things that make us grow—love, work, childbearing, art—require suffering in that broad sense. But every suffering can become a birth pain.

Thanatos, the death wish, impels us not forward but backward, back to the nearest any human will ever know of paradise on earth: the womb, where we had everything, supplied without our effort: no problems, no doubts, no worries about the future, because we couldn't think. We resent life, Freud said, for ejecting us out into the cold and noise and inconvenience, and we take revenge either by acting savagely or by pulling ourselves into cocoons where no one can get at us.

Our culture seems at first glance hellbent in pursuit of "the erotic," but not in Freud's sense. Clearly, our society isn't in pursuit of challenge but rather its opposite: *Thanatos,* the passive paradise of the womb. Even sex is often used not as a stimulant but as an anesthetic.

According to the National Assessment of Educational Progress, nearly half of high school *graduates* can't read at the 11th-grade level. In 1987, 27 percent of American high school students dropped out; in our nation's capital, it was 40 percent. Of those who stayed, the average senior spent 30 hours weekly on class and homework, while their Japanese counterparts spent 60 hours. In the first year 18-year-olds could vote, 50 percent did; in the 1988 presidential election, only 35 percent did. There's a lot of *Thanatos* going on out there!

When the Pilgrim in a man is dead (or suppressed out of fear), the self-deadening usually roots itself in the false belief, "Oh, well. I'm nobody." But that's a self-fulfilling prophecy. If you feel you're a nobody, you'll *act* like a nobody. Holden Caulfield simply couldn't face the challenge of becoming an adult *without* taking on the very shallow phoniness he hated in most adults. But refusing that challenge landed him in a mental hospital. As Carl Jung saw, neurosis is always the result of avoiding *legitimate* suffering. On the contrary, the Pilgrim in a young man rises to the ringing challenge that Jesse Jackson offers: to stand up and holler, "I . . . am . . . some body!"

Who were the people in the French and German undergrounds in World War II, who finally brought down the Berlin Wall, who stood unflinchingly in front of the tanks in Tienanmen Square? Who were Abraham Lincoln, Martin Luther King, Lech Walesa? All nobodies whose inner Pilgrim was ready when the lightning came. Who was Pope John XXIII? Just a fat little priest who had served most of his life in nowhere outposts, elected at an age close to Abraham's as a mere "curator" till a younger pope could be found. But he opened the windows on the musty Church and let in a hurricane that at least invited us to become a "Pilgrim Church."

When a man has access to his inner Pilgrim, he becomes a man of hope—which is quite different from optimism. Optimism can't see the cost with cautious and critical eyes; hope can. The courage of the hopeful man is coward's courage: honestly to say, "I *can't!* . . . But I'll try."

Without access to his inner Pilgrim—the *Eros* urge to reach out, to risk, to learn more, to change—a man becomes atrophied inside his defenses against challenge. His life isn't a coherent story line that's going someplace, but just ODTAA—One Damn Thing After Another, beads without a string. In older men, you see it in burnout, hopelessly dragging on with the job. In young men, you see it in "senioritis," putting the mind in neutral, doing the minimum, beating the system, getting a diploma without getting the education the diploma fraudulently testifies to. *Thanatos.* And even they, old or young, don't realize they're brain-dead and soul-starved.

One question to ask to see if a man's Pilgrim is still alive and receptive is to ask older men: "What were your dreams when you were 18? How has life skewed them—or fulfilled them beyond your hopes? Do you still find *zest* in your wife, your family, your job? If not, what would put it back?" If he wanted to be a great ballplayer, why not coach Little League? Maybe he once wanted to be an actor, but that was "foolish." Then why not join a community theater now?

Ask boys: "What kind of father do you want your children to have?" That man starts now. You can't fall into a kind of "moratorium" on growth between 12 and 22, when you go out for your first job, and expect to be instantly "ready" when the lightning stroke of fatherhood strikes. "What kind of job do you *want* to have—not just something to bring in the bucks but something to keep challenging your spirit?" If you wait till your senior year in college, you'll surely end up not with the job you want but with whatever job you can get, because Oz time is over.

If your inner Pilgrim resists challenge now, what concrete evidence do you have that some Fairy Godmother will show up, tap you with her magic wand, and suddenly activate it—with no effort or cooperation from you? If you balk at study now, who says you'll choose books over a beer blast in college? If school is dull routine now, what grounds do you have on which to base the hope the job you settle for will be any different? Think of it: a lifetime of mere survival.

THE PATRIARCH

Since the rise of the women's movement, the word "patriarch" has gotten a great deal of justified criticism. Agencies such as government, schools, business, education have been excessively patriarchal: men giving orders and women (and other men) submitting, even women smarter than those giving the orders. Like so many words knowledgeable people find offensive, "patriarch" has to be stripped of the negative, tyrannical elements offensive to women (and men, who are also its victims) *without* also stripping of its positive—in fact, essential—elements.

The tyrannical shadow side of the Patriarch results from assertiveness unchecked by real fatherlove (which is different from motherlove). We all know "patriarchal" men who are cold, demanding, crushing all opposing views, rigidly set against challenge or change, "laying burdens on others they do not carry themselves": Hitler, the Ayatollah, Saddam Hussein, down to the petty martinets who strangle us with red tape, puritanism, and "We've always done it this way."

But to limit "patriarch" to petty tyranny is to use only half the word and half the reality. The latter half, "arch," means *chief,* as in "archbishop, archangel, monarch." But the other half, "patri," means *father*, as in "paternal, patrimony, patriot." The tyrant leads without loving those he wants to save from themselves. A true Patriarch is a leader, but a loving man, too.

The Patriarch is responsible, like Abraham, not only to his clan but his neighbors. He was amazingly open-handed with Lot, offering whatever land he chose, and he himself would settle for the rest. He felt the irresistible need to rescue Lot when he was enslaved, to care for the needs of passing strangers, to haggle even with the Deity (!) on behalf of ten people in Sodom he didn't even know. Abraham was a kind man, treating all people as his *kinder* (children).

On the other hand, except for one lamentable occasion, Abraham did not treat people as if they were *childish*. He stepped in only when others were in *need* of his help. The good father is not one who does his son's homework or fights his battles, but he is there when the boy can't do it alone, when the boy needs a kind of tough love most mothers aren't encouraged to develop.

The good Patriarch leads without corralling, is willing to take the risk—and the heat if he is wrong—refuses to pass the buck to someone else or some agency. "Here I am. Send me." Such men go into politics, not to aggrandize themselves, but to help the helpless, to be agents of change, to care for the abused. They are doctors like Albert Schweitzer and Tom Dooley who give up lucrative practices to work for the helpless of Africa and Southeast Asia. Teachers and coaches who choose not to look for well-paying jobs in business or professional sports and prefer to help young people negotiate the trials of adolescence—usually with little thanks other than seeing at least some of their students become good people. You surely know a few.

Abraham's major failure, his shadow, came from passing the buck: Ishmael. His mistake (as with other good fathers) was in walking away from his major asset: compassionate decisiveness, leaving all the parenting to "the women." Many fathers are so concerned for the clan and the neighbors that they have no time for their own. Ishmael probably knew, to his sorrow, he was not conceived in love. He was summoned, without his choice, into a dysfunctional family, two battling mothers and a father busy with "more important things." None of us is born into a perfect family, and if we have no help in adjusting to imperfection, bitterness is our unwanted alternative. Abraham yielded his fatherhood in the name of peace in the house.

As a result, Ishmael suffered what the men's movement calls a "father wound," a feeling that even if his mother is for him, his father isn't, that he is not wanted, that he has no permanent hard place against which he can cling when the weather gets unbearable. He needs the assurance of his father until he can forge his own self-assurance. And in anger, Ishmael becomes "like a wild ass," macho, set against everyone, seeming to antagonize everyone, at least to get some attention.

Mythically, the story tries to show some basis for the antagonism between Israel, the children of Isaac, and the Arabs, the children of Ishmael. But it is as true of the "father-wounded" in our own city streets: the boys who go "wilding," gay-bashing, shooting indiscriminately at strangers in the streets. If you hurt the soul of a child, someone else will always pay.

It is easy to misread the sacrifice of Isaac as a kind of father-vendetta against the threatening son, like Darth Vader becoming the enemy of his son, Luke Skywalker. The father resents his son's claims on his own wife, the threat that the son will outdo him. Fathers "sacrifice" their sons to their careers or in wars for peace—or oil.

But that is to misread Abraham's story, using only one's psychiatric glasses, not one's theist glasses. From the first word, Abraham's is a story of trust, of being—no matter how patriarchal to other humans in need—"feminine" before God.

Sex is a matter of bodily fact: male or female. Gender is a matter of soul, the inner self: more "masculine" than "feminine," and vice versa. God at least seems to this author's experience to be more like an ideal (if unpredictable) Father than like the ideal (however assertive) Mother.

According to C.S. Lewis, God is the "absolute masculine"—*not* male, but the One who triggers birth and rebirth. Before God, all creatures are "feminine"—not passive, but receptive and creative. Though Lewis doesn't use it, the prototype is God's humble request to Mary— without whom God was "helpless," given the plan which required One fully God, yet fully human. Each day, then, God comes to us—male or female—and asks: "Please. Conceive my Son in you today."

So with Abraham. Every time God gave him the promise of descendents, he waited—25 years! Trusting. And that is the real meaning of God's pretense of wanting Isaac's life: to show not God but Abraham that God was still the most important person in Abraham's life.

Take an example of how we can deceive ourselves when we believe God is the focus of all reality and we do really love God "with your whole heart, your whole soul, and your whole mind." For 22 years I taught in a boys' school in upstate New York. I fully believed I was the world's luckiest man: working in a place I loved with people I loved. I had taught about 3,000 students, directed over 50 plays—both with students and with their parents. There were at least 50 homes I could walk into without even knocking. I was so busy all the time I had no time to pray, but I salved my conscience by saying to work is to pray.

Then out of nowhere, with no warning or discussion, I got a letter from my provincial transferring me to another school. I was more devastated even than at the deaths of my parents; for two days, practically the only thing I did was cry. It was as if my wife of 22 years suddenly said to me, "We've had a wonderful life all these years, but I'm divorcing you. No reason. We've just been together too long. Oh, by the way, you're now married to this woman in the Bronx." It wasn't a Shining Visitor, but since I had a vow of obedience, it surely was the voice of God.

Oh, I started to pray all right! Then on my annual retreat, like Abraham, I heard God saying, "Let go. I'll catch you." And I did. And God did. What God asked was: "Which is more important to you, really, in your heart of hearts: Me or that school and its people?" And the answer was painfully clear. No one said the truth would make you feel good, just set you free.

The lines that kept pursuing me through that retreat were the last two lines of John Donne's poem "Batter My Heart, Three-Personed God:" "And I, except you enthrall me, never shall be free, nor ever chaste except you ravish me." I'm here to serve, no matter what God asks. And if God asks, the least I can do is try, because without God I wouldn't be. Before God, all creation is "feminine;" in front of Jesus, we are his sheep; but before all others, we are "masculine;" we are *shepherds*, not sheep.

That is the role of the true inner Patriarch: to stand up and be counted, to clear the moneylenders out of the Temple, to challenge hypocritical pharisees, to try and try again to reason with the pig-headed and, yes, perhaps even to be crucified for our troubles. And not just once.

Any young man's inner Pilgrim and Patriarch are potentials awaiting activation.

The question to ask your inner Pilgrim to see if it is alive and well: Do you really *want* to be challenged, or would you prefer just to be "unbothered," pretending you need challenge? We all *claim*, for instance, that we want "a good education." But is that really true? What you *do* shouts so loudly we can't even hear what you claim. When you travel to and from school, what's in your pocket: a paperback or a Walkman? Do you always do an outline for big papers? Or do you do "just the written stuff," ask for extensions, sweet-talk the teacher into a D? Is it possible you tell your-self lies about yourself and, worse, end up believing them?

The question to ask your inner patriarch: Do you genuinely feel responsibility for those around you? Your family and friends, of course, but your classmates? Your teachers? The people who clean up your messes in the cafeteria? If you found yourself with an unarguably ineffective teacher, what would you do about it? If you went to the administration and nothing was done, what would you do then?

If being a Christian Patriarch and Pilgrim is boring, I don't know what could be called interesting.

For further discussion see the appendix,
pages 177–179.

3 MOSES:
WARRIOR / MAGICIAN

Once upon a time in Egypt there lived a wicked pharaoh named Seti who vowed to immortalize his name by building more cities than any monarch ever. But after awhile his taxes had bled the citizens so dry he feared a revolution. So he found a solution: the Hebrews, who were not only rich but multiplied like rats.

"Round them up!" cried Seti. "Man, woman, and brat! Confiscate their goods!" So they herded all Hebrews into camps, to work and starve building Pharaoh's monuments.

But the more Seti persecuted them, the more resilient they became. The fittest survived and produced more and more strong-bodied and strong-willed children. Finally Seti could take no more. "Every newborn Hebrew boy," he cried, "into the Nile!"

At that time, a Hebrew woman named Jochebed had a son she vowed to save. So she put the child in a tar-slicked basket and pushed him out through the reeds into the channel of the Nile and set his older sister, Miriam, nearby to watch. Just then, Pharoah's daughter came down to the Nile to bathe and noticed the floating basket and sent her slave girls to fetch it. The baby's sister Miriam pushed forward and said, "Forgive me, my lady. A nurse?" And off she went to get Jochebed, to nurse him. When the boy was weaned, his mother brought him to the princess, who said, "He will be Moses, born out of water."

Moses grew up the adopted son of a princess. But he knew. Almost against his will, he began to haunt the building sites where his people groaned like beasts. Then one day, he saw an Egyptian guard beat a Hebrew slave to death. Incensed, he strangled the guard, heaping sand over his corpse to hide it. But next day, drawn back, hoping the wind had not blown the sand away, he found two Hebrews fighting. "Stop!" he cried. "Why beat another Hebrew?" The man sneered. "You going to kill *me* the way you killed that guard yesterday?" Moses' heart clutched. And he ran, away from the construction site, out of the city gates toward the Sinai desert.

There, he attached himself to a herdsman named Jethro, and after awhile he married Jethro's daughter, Zipporah. Days eased into years, and Moses settled into the routine of leading Jethro's sheep to graze in the moonscape wilderness. One day, watching dust devils rise into the shimmering heat, Moses saw a scrubby bush. At first, he thought the sun behind the bush made it seem to blaze. Then, in terror, he realized the sun was at his back. Cautiously, he moved closer.

From within the blaze a voice cried: "Moses!"

"Y-Y-Yes. Here I am." And Moses covered his face, terrified to look at God.

"You have forgotten your people back in Egypt," God said. "I have not. They cry, day after day, yearning to be freed. I have heard them. And I am sending someone to lead my people out of his slave camps." The voice of God became very quiet. "I'm sending you."

"But . . . but . . . ," Moses stammered, "I . . . I'm nobody. How . . . ?"

"I will be with you," the Lord said.

"But really," Moses cringed, "let's say I . . . I walk in and say, 'Oh, uh, *God* sent me to set you free,' they'll laugh at me. They'll ask me, 'What God? What is this God's name?'"

"I AM!" the Lord thundered. "HE WHO CAUSES TO BE sends you! The Lord. God of Abraham, Isaac, and Jacob. I will lead them back into the land I gave Abraham. Tell Pharaoh 'The Hebrew God commands you: Let my people go.'"

But Moses stammered, "L-L-Lord G-G-God, *please!* I'm not a good speaker. And . . . and talking to you hasn't made me any better at it. I . . . " The bush blazed brighter, and Moses fell back. "Who gives a man his mouth?" the Lord thundered. *"I* do! Now go! I will teach you what to say." But Moses persisted. "Someone else!" The Lord took a deep breath. "All right. Aaron, your brother, is a good speaker. Tell him what to say. Now . . . *go!"*

So Moses gathered his wife and children and set out with them for Egypt. When they returned to the slave camps, Seti had died, and his son, Ramses, had taken his place, an iron-souled man who dreamed of more and more buildings, no matter how many slaves it cost. So the Hebrews were ripe for Moses' message, and they truly believed the Lord had heard their cries.

Moses and Aaron sought audience with Pharaoh. Moses nudged Aaron, and Aaron spoke. "The Lord says, 'Let my people go!'" Ramses sneered. "What? Who is this . . . Lord? I don't know any 'Lord.' Go away." But Moses whispered, and Aaron said, "Our God tells us to journey into the desert to offer sacrifice, or Egypt will be crushed." Pharaoh shouted, "Back to work! You're more numerous than the Egyptians and eat twice as much. Now you want to stop work? Out!" When they left, Ramses gave orders to work the Hebrews twice as hard as before.

So the people flared at Moses, "They'll kill us! It's all your fault." So Moses complained to the Lord. "See what you've made me do?" he cried. "Sent me here to make things worse! Fine help you've been!" But the Lord whispered, "Wait. Before long, he will *force* my people out. Go again." Moses grumped. "Why? Even the *Hebrews* won't listen! Why should he? I *told* you I was a p-p-poor . . . " But the Lord said only, *"I have spoken!"*

Next day, Moses and Aaron crept to the Nile as Ramses was about to bathe and Aaron raised his staff. Instantly, the Nile turned to blood, and all the streams that fed it ran bloody. Fish came belly-up, stinking. But Ramses turned away angrily. And the Nile ran blood for seven days.

Then an infestation of frogs tumbled from every river and pool and well, the land covered with slimy, hopping green blobs, even in the pharaoh's palace and bed. Pharaoh summoned Moses and said, "Enough! Pray to this . . . this Lord of yours to take away these frogs. And I will let you go into the desert to offer your damnable sacrifice!" So Moses prayed and every frog died. But when Pharaoh was rid of the pests, he smiled and refused to live up to his promise.

And so it went. First the country was overwhelmed with gnats. Then animals and people bristled with boils, but Pharaoh held firm. Then hail riddled the land, then locusts ate everything the hail had left. The Lord said to Moses, "In the evening of the fourteenth day, dress for travel; kill a yearling and splash its blood on your doorposts; roast it and eat it quickly, standing, staffs in your hands. This is the Passover of the Lord. That night, I will slaughter every firstborn male, human or animal, but I will pass over doors daubed with the blood of the Passover animal."

The night air over Egypt was heavy with wailing, mothers rocking the corpses of their firstborn sons, and there was no Egyptian house without its dead. So Pharaoh called Moses and growled, "Out. Every last one of you. Just . . . be gone!"

So, before dawn, after years in servitude, thousands of Hebrews set out with their flocks in a long trek toward the desert and, beyond it, to Canaan. But yet again Ramses changed his mind. So he called for his warriors and chariots and set off in pursuit of the triumphant Hebrews.

Just as they came to the Red Sea, worrying how they could cross, the Hebrews saw a cloud of dust in the air behind them, and they were terrified. They ran to Moses and cried, "Were there no graves in Egypt that you brought us out here to die in the desert?" But the Lord whispered to Moses, "Raise your staff over the sea!" And as Moses did, a hurricane blew from the east, sending water flying up into huge palisades, and a canyon of dry land opened between the waves, and the people marched through it.

Just as the Egyptians had plunged into the watery canyon, the Lord flashed horrific lightning over their heads. Horses panicked, and chariots careened, locking wheels and tossing charioteers like rag dolls into the air. Then Moses raised his staff, and the winds suddenly stood still. The watery walls crumbled, tons of water crashing down on the screaming men and horses. And the baffled Hebrews turned and made their way out into the wilderness of rock and sand.

Two months dragged by, the Hebrews grumbling and blundering along. Finally, on the first day of their third month of wandering, they arrived at the mountain called Sinai, and there they camped. And Moses went up the mountain to meet with God.

Suddenly the air was thick with thunder, and clouds around the mountain were savage with lightning, and all the people in the camp trembled. And God spoke to Moses, swearing a covenant between the Lord and his people, pledging himself to them as to his only wife. The Lord would be faithful to them and they to him and his Law. In that moment, Israel was born.

Male Archetypes in MOSES

	Archetype	Shadow	Balance
Warrior	Courageous confidence	Self-serving; bullying	A code of honor
Magician	Intuitive inventiveness	Cunning egotism	Humility

WARRIOR

What Jesus is to the New Testament, Moses is to the Old Testament; the Exodus from Egypt is to Jews what the resurrection is to Christians; their Passover has become our Easter.

The Warrior, as Moses proved himself—reluctantly—to be, is a fundamental male archetype. It's bred into a man's soul from the days when we actually were warriors and hunters. Like the Patriarch, the Warrior in a male has its shadow side: Pharaoh. Just as the unloving Patriarch can become a tyrant, the Warrior—unchecked by his Anima—becomes a macho bully, like Ishmael. We see them in our own streets: Hell's Angels, pimps, pushers. We see them in the corridors of power: the military-industrial complex, the battling emirs of the Middle East, the bully boys on both sides in Northern Ireland.

On the positive side, however, the Warrior battles disease, corruption, ignorance, crime, drugs. The difference is what the released Warrior in a man fights for and against. The shadow of the Warrior fights for himself—often claiming he does it for others. The true Warrior fights for the oppressed. Mohandas Gandhi and Martin Luther King, Jr., were not peacemakers; they were men of bravery, self-sacrifice, and endurance who refused to be willing victims, refused to say, "Oh, what good would it do?" They came forward and kept on demanding, "Let my people go!"

The inner Warrior defends a man's soul-boundaries. It gives a man a sense of self-esteem and integrity he simply will *not* allow to be violated. Eleanor Roosevelt once said you can never be degraded without your cooperation. Often, as with Gandhi and King—and Jesus—the Warrior's weapon is not sword or fists but silence, refusing to turn rage into a weapon and put it into his oppressor's hand. But there is a great difference between silent endurance in a no-win situation and mere sheeplike yielding to exploitation from fear of the cost: embarrassment, rejection, jeers.

The difference between the Warrior and the bully is the true Warrior has a *code*. In T. H. White's *The Once and Future King*, Lancelot, Arthur's greatest warrior, "tried to have a Word. . . . His Word was valuable to him not only because he was good, but also because he was bad."

A man's *word* is the measure of his character; when you say, "I give you my word . . . ," you are pledging your *self*, your soul, your integrity—that is, the *wholeness* of your self. Thomas More, in Robert Bolt's play, "A Man for All Seasons," says that when a man takes an oath, he's holding his soul in his hands like holding water in his hands. If he opens his fingers, how will he ever get his soul back? And he found he couldn't affix his name to the oath declaring Henry VIII head of the Church in England. His name—a mere configuration of ink on a document! But in putting his name on the line, he was putting *himself*—his soul—on the line. Because he refused, he was beheaded. His soul was more important to him than life, because it *was* his life.

Unlike a child, when a true man makes a promise, that promise is a *commitment* he will honor, no matter how inconvenient, no matter whether a more enticing alternative arises.

Three times a year when I begin tryouts for a play, I have each boy and girl fill out a sheet asking various questions like name, school, year, and so forth. But there is a statement that, if chosen for the cast, each one promises to be there when needed, prepared and cooperative, and it ends: "I consider this a commitment," and asks for the

student's signature. Then, when a student fails to show
(dentist's appointment, my girlfriend was sick), I call and
ask why they missed rehearsal. You gave me your word.
"No, I didn't." Yes. You signed your *name*; that's your word.
If you don't honor what your word promised, your word is
worth *nothing*. (I have had the same argument with over-
protective parents, whose arguments prove they're not
adults either.)

Would an adult *man* try to weasel out of a commitment?
Would an adult man lie in a trivial but tight situation (especially to his parents to whom he owes everything)? Would
an adult man cheat on a quiz or test that in a month he'll
forget he even took, dream up excuses for work not done,
ask for an extension?

Perhaps that is *the* test of whether you are an adult male
or merely a grown-up child: How good is your word?

Practitioners of the martial arts bow to the truth of
their own inner weaknesses and thus train not only the
body but the soul, which must control what it allows that
well-trained body to do: *never* to act blindly or out of anger
or need for revenge, and *always* to take full responsibility
for whatever you have done.

The God who has no patience with complacency finds
Moses settled into the comforting routine of herding sheep
and presents a most disconcerting invitation: You are to
lead a warrior crusade against Pharaoh to make him let my
people go. Little wonder Moses stammers for quite some
time his objections to that little plan. But God promises to
be his teacher, as Obiwan Kenobi and Yoda the Jedi Knight
were for Luke Skywalker. And Moses marches tremulously
toward this cosmic battle armed only with his staff. It is
Yahweh who will do the fighting.

We see the same reluctance for heroism in Peter, the
fisherman. "Lord, depart from me. I'm a sinful man." But
when the Lord has plans for you, all protests of unworthi-
ness are futile. You're dealing with a God who had no

problem creating a universe out of nothing. And later, when Jesus comes walking across the water to Peter's boat, Peter finds that out. As long as he keeps his eyes only on Jesus, he can do what in his "saner" moments he would consider idiotic. Perhaps Peter didn't literally walk on water, but the Coward of Good Friday did become a martyr.

MAGICIAN

As the Warrior is merely a channel for God's power, so the Magician is only a conduit for God's control over nature. We can serve God's purposes best with our wits rather than with weapons.

The Magician is a man in full control of his wits, not merely the analytical power of his left brain but also the intuitive power of his right brain. The Magician follows his hunches, his gut intuition. "Maybe," the awakened Magician says, "if we fool around with this bread mold, we can come up with some kind of medicine." And penicillin is born. "I wonder what we might be able to finagle out of these intriguing silicon chips." And the whole world is changed. Martin Luther King, Jr., was a magician of words to stir the human heart, and thus a nobody preacher from a little nowhere Alabama church changed the history of the world. The true Magician is in touch with the power and the mind of God.

To test what shape your inner Magician is in, ask yourself how you usually react to: "We've always done it this way," or "You ask too many questions," or "Everybody says . . . " On a rainy Saturday, little kids whine, "Mommy, there's nothing to *do!*" What would an adult man do with a long stretch of dull time? What would an adult man do with a school subject he finds tedious—but inescapable? How good is your imagination?

There is a shadow side of a man's Magician. Unchecked by humility—by the realization one serves rather than dominates—the Magician begins to believe *he* is the source of his own power, rather than an instrument in the hands of God. You see the shadow in Adolf Hitler who, like Martin Luther King, could bring people to their feet with the magic of his words. You see it far too often in televangelists who start out, most times, sincerely preaching the word of God, but their success—especially their financial success—goes to their heads, and they disgrace themselves, preaching generosity, chastity, and honesty but practicing something quite different.

St. Paul, who was no mean magician of words himself, speaks of a time when he was carried out of himself in a vision of God. He wanted to boast of his blessing, but "to keep me from being bloated with pride, I was given 'a thorn in the flesh,' which acts as Satan's messenger when I'm tempted to be proud." (2 Corinthians 12:8-9) Paul never says what that "thorn" literally was, perhaps just as well, because it allows us to empathize—each in his own uniquely individual way—with someone called to greatness yet painfully aware of his own shortcomings. Each of us, if he is honest, has his "thorn." As long as we keep going to confession, we can preserve our inner Magician from arrogance. Bad people don't go to confession; only good people do.

Abraham and Sarah were very old, yet God rooted the entire nation of Israel, 3,000 years of men and women, in their barren loins. Moses stammered, afraid of public speaking and unwilling to accept the dubious honor of facing down Pharaoh and founding a new people. Peter was a sinner, a fumbler, a coward; Paul was a persecutor of the infant Church, yet nonetheless look what God made of them—once they were willing to get out of God's way and be used.

As God told Paul when he inflicted the "thorn in his flesh," "My power is strongest in your weakness."

One begins to sense a pattern here.

One's Warrior and Magician are also potentials which need not be activated. Ask of your inner Warrior: What are you willing to stand up and fight for—not with your fists but with your words and your wits? Dr. Martin Luther King, Jr., said that anyone who didn't have something in life worth dying for didn't deserve to live. Other than your family and friends, what would you "die" for—again, not literally, but at least take the risk of looking the fool in front of your friends? If you see a few older boys humiliating a younger boy, for instance, do you step in and stop it? Or do you just distract yourself and move on?

Ask your inner Magician: Do you really sense the *power* in you to change things? And do you sense that, whatever you think of your shortcomings, an all-powerful God thinks you're still worthy to be his son and his emissary? If you know someone, for instance, who always eats lunch alone, do you even suspect you could bring him or her more alive, make him or her feel respected?

The only one who can smother your power and magic is you.

For further discussion see the appendix, pages 179–180.

4 JONATHAN:
FRIEND

Once upon a time there was this hill chieftain named Saul, a conniver with the temper of a hornet, who itched to be the first Hebrew King. Now, after the pharaohs in Egypt, Hebrews were not overly fond of kings. They had only one king: HE WHO CAUSES TO BE. Father-chieftains like Abraham could resolve their squabbles. But from the north came an invasion of Philistines, with the newest kind of arms: iron. So Saul saw his chance and grabbed it. He united all the tribes to batter the Philistines back. And in the flush of victory, Saul had himself anointed king.

Once Saul's army was armed with iron, he was everywhere successful—to the point he began to erect monuments to himself. The Lord was not pleased. He sent his prophet, Samuel, to Bethlehem where a man named Jesse lived with his eight sons. The Lord would show Samuel which son he wished anointed king in Saul's place. When Jesse introduced his eldest, Eliab, the young man was so strong and handsome, Samuel was certain he would be the Lord's choice. But he wasn't. One by one Jesse's sons came to meet Samuel, but each time the Lord was silent.

"Is that all?" Samuel asked. "There is one other," Jesse smiled. "The runt of the litter. He's tending the sheep. I'll send for him, but . . . " When the boy came shyly to Samuel's presence, the prophet felt the voice of the Lord whisper, "He's the one." The boy's name was David.

So David came to Saul's court, a lively boy who captured all hearts, even King Saul, who had become victim of unpredictable foul moods. Only David's harp and songs could calm the ornery old man. And Saul was pleased David and his favorite son, Jonathan, became fast friends.

Some time after, the Philistines again attacked, but this time with another secret weapon: a giant named Goliath, over seven feet tall, covered with a hundred pounds of armor, who challenged the Hebrews to single combat— winner take all. The bravest of Saul's warriors saw such an encounter was a wasted suicide, since accepting the hopeless challenge was equivalent to handing the kingdom to the Philistines. Saul offered a huge reward, marriage to his daughter, and a promise the hero would live forever tax free. No inducement produced a doomed hero.

Just then, David arrived at the camp with food for his brothers. When he heard the challenge, he presented himself to the king and offered to accept it. Saul scoffed, "You're just a boy! This giant has been a soldier all his life." David persisted. "And I have been a shepherd all my life," he said. "When a wolf or a bear threatened my sheep, I stunned it with my slingshot then beat it to death." So Saul relented and even gave David his own armor. But when the boy tried to walk, he couldn't, so he peeled off the bronze, and strode out against Goliath just as he was.

Goliath's laughter shook the trees all round the field. "What?" he howled. "Am I a dog that they send a boy to tame me? Ha! I'll cut off your head and feed it to the crows!" But David said, "You're armed with a sword, but I'm armed with the power of the Lord!" And the boy ran at him, whirling his sling, and let fire. The rock struck the giant in the center of his forehead, and over he went, stunned. David struggled to heft the giant's sword and brought it crashing down on his neck. The Philistines were paralyzed for a moment, then remembered their feet and ran howling away, the men of Israel and Judah crying at their heels.

Rather than resenting his friend's sudden adoration by the crowds, Jonathan was David's most fervent admirer. Before the returning soldiers lifted David to their shoulders, Jonathan gave his friend his sword and bow, and the two swore eternal friendship. In all future battles each young man fought fearlessly, knowing his back was protected by his unquestionable friend.

Battle after battle, the two covered themselves with honor, and the soldiers idolized David. But when they returned, women greeted them singing, "Saul has killed his thousands, but David his tens of thousands." And the king was listening. Day by day, his jealousy and hatred for David grew. Saul sent David on suicidal missions, but each time David returned triumphant.

Jonathan tried to calm his father, but Saul shouted, "Fool! Do you think the people will give you the throne while that man lives?" Jonathan said if David would be a better king, he should have the throne. But Saul went on swearing he would have no peace while David lived.

When Jonathan told David his fears, David laughed. "What have I done?" he asked. "I've risked my life again and again for your father." But Jonathan was certain. So David said, "Let's test it. Tomorrow is the New Moon Feast. Tell your father my family has begged me to celebrate the feast with them. When I'm not in my place, the king will either accept the reason—and we will know I'm safe—or he will throw one of his foul fits—and we will know I must run for my life."

David would hide himself in rocks above the place the young prince practiced archery. If Jonathan told the boy who fetched his spent arrows, "Come back, you've gone too far," then David would be safe to return. If he called out, "No, you must go further," David must flee.

When the king saw David's place at the feast empty, he flew into a towering rage. "You care more for him than for your own father! And your king!" When Jonathan tried to protest, Saul cried out and hurled his spear at his son, and Jonathan fled for his life.

The following day, Jonathan climbed to the archery field where David crouched hidden among the rocks. The prince fired an arrow far beyond the boy who waited to fetch it. "No!" Jonathan shouted. "Go much farther away!" And David fled.

For the next few years, David and his band of followers roamed the hills, living a Robin Hood life, defending the helpless and avenging the exploited. When Saul returned from his latest conflict with the marauding Philistines, he heard David was encamped near Engedi, so he set out with his army to capture and kill him. As they reached the White Goat Rocks, Saul called a halt for his weary men, and he himself went into a huge cave to rest in the cool shade.

Unbeknownst to him, David and his men were hiding in the depths of that very cave. "This is your chance," the men whispered. But David said, "The Lord anointed Saul my king. He's treated me cruelly and unfairly. But he is my friend's father." Instead, David crawled quietly to the sleeping king and cut off the corner of his robe, then crept back into the darkness.

Saul got up and left the cave, leading his men off into the wilderness. But while Saul was still within earshot, David stood in the mouth of the cave and shouted, "My father! Why do you believe I want to harm you and take your throne? We were in the cave all the time you slept. My men wanted me to kill you, but I told them I would never harm you. Look," he said, holding up the piece of Saul's robe, "I was this close to you with my sword!"

Saul stood, shocked. "Is it really you, David, my son?" And Saul began to weep. "You are right, and I am wrong. Today you spared my life. How can a man spare his enemy? I will never harm you again." And Saul and his troops marched away.

Years later, Saul and his sons had a final clash with the Philistines on Mount Gilboa. It was a catastrophic encounter. Saul and his sons were surrounded, each badly wounded. Saul begged his armor bearer to finish him off with his sword, lest he fall into the hands of the Philistines. When the young man refused, Saul fell on his own sword and died. In the same battle, David's faithful friend, Jonathan, also perished.

When David heard the news, he sang a lament:

> *Saul and Jonathan, so precious to me,*
> *Together in life, together in death,*
> *Swifter than eagles, stronger than lions.*
> *I grieve for Jonathan, my friend,*
> *Dearer to me than life itself.*

Male Archetypes in JONATHAN

	Archetype	Shadow	Balance
Friend	*Loyalty*	*Dependency; domination*	*Ability to stand alone*

FRIEND

What makes David and Jonathan true friends and Saul a false friend is that both David and Jonathan rejoice in the depth of their friendship, but neither *needs* the other to be a self. Jonathan is loyal to David, even in the face of his father's unjust threats; David is loyal to Saul at the very moment Saul seeks with an army to slaughter him, and he adamantly refuses to kill the king because the man is his friend's father. Saul is no friend because *he* insists on being the focus of the lives of those he claims to love. He is jealous of David's popularity—where a true friend, like Jonathan, rejoices for it; Saul is jealous of his son's affection for their friend, reading every honest loyalty which excludes him as a treachery and betrayal. Friendships can't be one-way streets.

If one friend can't function without the other, can't focus their profoundest affections on their wives and families (without losing affection for one another), the relationship wouldn't be a true friendship but an enslavement. If one friend can't tolerate his friend's other friends, it is just as clearly an attempt at control. True friends allow their friends to be enriched by as many others as possible, because honest love means setting those one loves free. As the old saying goes, "Set those you love free. If they come back to you, they're yours; if not, they never were."

I have attended at least 100 graduations, and at each one—without fail—the valedictorian places the strongest emphasis in his or her talk on the crucial importance of the friendships the students have enriched themselves with during the past four years. I have no doubt they are sincere or that their friends are truly precious to them. But I find myself shaking my head, remembering how many times in their senior year I've begged them to break out of their little cliques and enrich themselves with *more* friends. How can you have too many friends?

In the school where I teach, I find the richest social and ethnic mix I have found in any school. Half the students come from the lower-to-middle-class Bronx, the other half from middle-class-to-luxury Westchester. In every class group, two or three Orientals, three or four blacks (some West Indian, some African), four or five Hispanics (from various countries), Italians, Irish, Poles, Bronx yuppies, Westchester yuppies. In class, we all get along fine. But in the cafeteria? Another story. Blacks sit with blacks, Orientals with Orientals, Hispanics with Hispanics, white yuppies from one affluent suburb insulated from some other affluent suburb's yuppies.

The principal reason, I think, is fear of the cost. After a couple years I've got a few tested friends. That's enough. Why risk involvement with somebody who might be a leech or a bore?

Each year I hold a class where I have students play the game of Trust: One person stands behind the other with strict instruction to protect the other when he falls back. Without fail, the person falling crooks his head over his shoulder "just in case" someone's pulling a trick. Boys who can skate 70 miles an hour without fear of being checked into the boards are tense as rabbits. Why? Because the hockey player is in *control;* the faller is dependent on someone he finds it difficult to trust—even when the catcher has been, to that moment, his best friend.

If you are afraid to take risks, you will have few friends.

THE PROGRESS OF FRIENDSHIP

Picture a circle about a yard in diameter, say, on a chalkboard. In your imagination, write outside the circle: ANONYMOUS. Beyond the thin membrane of the circle are all those people you've never met (and are not likely to). Everyone inside the circle is someone you at least "sort of" know, from ACQUAINTANCES (a face you recognize, but little more), to FRIENDS (those people you wouldn't mind sitting with in the cafeteria), to PALS (those you simply expect to sit with), and finally to BEST FRIENDS (those who'll probably be ushers at your wedding).

Think about your best friend, someone you'd risk your safety or your acceptability for. At one time, that person was out there in the ANONYMOUS wilderness. What was the *very* first step that finally brought that person into the innermost BEST circle? Not being introduced, not saying hello, not getting to know him. (Why is that question so difficult? We've all been through it. I'm not asking you to explain the quantum theory.)

The first step is to *notice* him. Unless you notice him—fixate him out of the faceless, anonymous crowd—there's no chance of your ever becoming acquainted, much less best friends. Each person out there has the potential to be a best friend, just as your best friends once were. But we *shield* ourselves from knowing other people, not just by ethnic or racial or social prejudice, but because we're unaware they're even *there*. To test the truth of that assertion, try an experiment: In your next break from class (or the office), walk to your next destination and really *look* at every face you can vacuum in. Count how many about whom you say, "I have *never* seen that face before." All those potential enrichments washing past like air.

How does someone move from becoming merely an ACQUAINTANCE ("Oh, yeah, I know who he is") to being a FRIEND—not someone you'd open your secrets to, just someone you don't feel uncomfortable with? It takes time and talk. Surely not profound; just chit-chat. But there's a conversation *beneath* the chit-chat; it says, "I'm at ease with you."

Further, how does someone move from FRIEND to PAL, someone you're not only easy with but count on? Usually, you've shared something together *beyond* time and talk, something important: day after day of butt-busting practice, meeting a deadline, hoping the other actor remembers his lines. There's a solid base of experience that grounds my belief: "I can trust him."

Finally, how does one move from trustworthy, comfortable PAL to BEST FRIEND? One boy put it better than anyone else ever has, at least to me: "You can cry and not be afraid." You invite a very good friend "inside" your inner self, let him see all the warts and knobs, and he comes out saying, "So what? We're still friends." If you have someone like that in your life, grapple him to your heart with hoops of steel. You will never find any greater treasure.

I think we "learn" more about male bonding from movies than we learn from reflecting on our own experience of it. We see guys in the movies and on TV who are obviously, unquestionably macho. It's a false image. They're pals, all right, but have they shared their *weakness?* Does Rambo have a trusted sidekick? Does Conan the Barbarian or the characters Tom Cruise or Eddie Murphy play? Their expression of affection is a poke in the face. John Wayne had followers, but they were subservient, ready to do his will; not friends but hangers-on.

Each of us, at the deepest level of our souls (therefore at the deepest level of what makes us adults vs. grown-ups), responds to the images of manhood projected to us. Men are self-reliant ("We don't need no stinkin' bodges!"); they don't feel or cry (Batman is always masked); they don't touch, because touch is always sexual (except when scoring a goal); they are task-oriented and competitive (even marriage and family are "tasks" to be "mastered"). A false image of men.

Because of this macho image projected in the Playboy-Rambo media, boys measure themselves against a distorted standard. Anything that jars with the dominating, tough, inflexible male standard (like vulnerability, the urge for self-disclosure, the need to grieve: the Anima) is not only "unacceptable" to one's peers but perhaps also reason to doubt the "purity" of one's male sexuality. Another test: Think of your best male friend, someone to whom you could reveal your worst fears, sure that you'd still be friends after. Now, in the quiet of your own mind, where no one else can hear, can you say, "I love him"? If not, there's something *really* wrong with your idea of love.

Off-handed touch, genuine affection, and love are *not* symptoms of homosexuality. They are elements of a well-rounded male character. Without them, a man is as soulless as brass.

KINDS OF FRIENDS

To live male life to the fullest, a man needs (at least) three kinds of true friends: a mentor, a companion, and (for want of a better word) a protegé. Perhaps it will help to understand if we look at three staunch friends in the New Testament: Paul, Barnabas, and Timothy.

Each one of us needs a friend like Paul, an older man who is willing to share his experience with us—in the first place, to help us not to make the same mistakes he made, and in the second place, to help the older man's mistakes have value. The mentor needn't be educated (though that helps), but he does need to have been around the track a few times. He needs to be both strong and vulnerable, willing to exert tough love when it's called for, willing to share his past and present weaknesses.

Each one of us needs a friend like Barnabas, a companion, a soul-brother, who, as Howard Hendricks puts it, "loves you but is not impressed by you." In Acts, Barnabas was the disciple who mediated the case of Saul (Paul), the former persecutor of Christians, against the understandable suspicions of the Jerusalem church when Saul tried to convince them God had called him to be one of them. He and Paul were the first agents sent out into the Gentile world, roving from place to place around the Mediterranean, founding new communities of Christians. In Lycaonia, the two were such impressive speakers that the pagans called Barnabas Zeus because he was apparently so imposing, and called Saul Hermes, "because he did all the talking."

It is interesting to note that at the outset of their voyages, the author of Acts consistently writes "Barnabas and Saul" went to such-and-such place; then abruptly he changes to "Paul and Barnabas," indicating a reversal of leadership after Paul was no longer a newcomer. Yet Barnabas seems content with the change, just as Jonathan was content that David outshone him.

Every man needs a Barnabas who will not only cherish him but also challenge him. Just as Paul confronted Peter, Barnabas confronted Paul when Paul rejected a young man named John Mark who Paul felt had betrayed him. A genuine friend can call his friend up short without fear of rejection, willing to put up with his friend's momentary anger because he trusts in the depth of the friendship: "You know, you're drinking too much; I think what you said to him was mean-spirited; Have you lost your pride or something; Give me your car keys." Such a friend is beyond price.

Each of us needs a friend like Timothy, Paul's pupil. He was the son of a Greek father and a Jewish mother whom Paul converted on his first visit to Lystra in Asia Minor. The next time Paul passed through, Timothy went along with him. Although he was quite young, timid, and in ill health, Paul still sent him as his legate on difficult missions. Later, he appointed Timothy bishop of the churches in Ephesus, where Paul wrote him two letters of advice, and Paul mentions this young apostle in five other letters. In 1 Timothy, Paul addresses him affectionately: "Timothy, because of our faith, you are like a son to me."

Just as every man (no matter how old) needs a mentor to challenge him to keep growing, so also every man (no matter how young) needs someone for whom he himself can act as a mentor. Even in high school, a boy can volunteer tutor a younger boy. In college, he can become a Big Brother. It might seem like a small contribution, but think of it: A fatherless boy, with no positive male presence in his life, perhaps thinking there is no hope for him in school, no future except a life on the streets—suddenly made to feel he's important to someone he respects. It's a challenge one male can offer to another—the older boy challenging the younger. And vice versa.

Loving

Probably no word in any language is more misused than "love": "I'd love a pizza; I love what you've done to this room; I'd love to punch that guy in the puss." In none of those cases does the speaker really mean love: enjoy, appreciate, take wicked pleasure in. So-called love songs aren't about love; they're about being *in* love, romance, panting breath, and thumping hearts.

That's one of the reasons so many boys are afraid to say they love their best male friends. "Love," in their minds, is all tangled up with sexual overtones.

Genuine love is not a feeling; it's an act of will, a *commitment*, that takes over when the feelings fail, when the friend is no longer even *likable*. When a parent disciplines an uncooperative child, when a teacher gives a lazy student an F, when a friend tells a friend he's in the wrong, that's an act of genuine love. It says, "I don't care if you hate me right now, because I love you."

The best test I know of genuine love comes from St. Paul:

> Love is always patient and kind; it is never
> jealous; love is never boastful or conceited; it is
> never rude or selfish; it does not take offense,
> and is not resentful. Love takes no pleasure in

others' sins but delights in the truth; love is always ready to excuse, to trust, to hope, and to endure whatever comes. Love never comes to an end (1 Corinthians 13:4–8).

For further discussion see the appendix, pages 180–182.

5 SOLOMON: _KING_

After Saul's death David seized the throne and annihilated all Saul's relatives to protect himself against rivals to the throne. All in all, hero though he was, David was a corruptible man. Yet he moved the government south to Jerusalem, organized administration and taxation, formed an army that broadened the borders of Israel enormously, and began at Jerusalem a city to rival the great cities of Egypt.

And when David died after ruling Israel 40 years, he passed the throne to his son, Solomon, who "had it all:" looks, warlike skills, and—something rare in Hebrew kings—brains. One day, as Solomon offered sacrifice, the Lord appeared to him as in a dream. "What would you ask me?" God said. And Solomon knelt and answered, "Lord God, I am young and don't know how to rule. Give me wisdom to rule your people with justice." And the Lord said, "Because you asked for wisdom to rule justly—not long life or riches or the death of your enemies—I will do as you ask. You will have more understanding and compassion than anyone has ever had." And the Lord God faded back into the mists of the dream.

Soon after, two prostitutes came before King Solomon for judgment. Each had given birth to baby boys. "One night," one said, "that other one turned over in bed and smothered her child. She put her dead baby next to me while I slept and took my boy into her bed." But the second snapped, "No! The living child is mine! The dead baby is hers!" So Solomon called his guard. "Take your sword and cut the child in two; give each woman half." The second woman was content. But the first threw herself at Solomon's feet. "No! Don't kill the child! Give it to her!" So Solomon gave the first woman her child and punished the other. And when the people of Israel heard of King Solomon's decision, they knew the Lord God was guiding their king.

Now Solomon's father, David, had extended the borders of Israel from the Euphrates River in the east to the borders with Egypt in the west, and all the petty kings were now subject to King Solomon, sending tribute to Jerusalem every month, so the Hebrews had become a wealthy nation. At last, throughout the land there was peace and prosperity, so Solomon decided it was time the people constructed an enormous temple in which the Lord might dwell in their midst. So, 480 years after the people had left Egypt, Solomon began the work, and after 13 years, it was finished. The box in which the Ten Commandments rested, the symbol of the presence of the Lord God among them, was carried in solemn procession into the innermost room, the Holy of Holies.

The Lord God appeared to Solomon and said, "If the people remain faithful, I will dwell in this house forever. But if they stray into serving other gods, I will abandon them, and the people of Israel will be carried off in servitude. This Temple will be a ruin, the home of jackals and dust blown by the wind."

Kings and queens from all over came to marvel at Solomon's Temple, his palace, his wealth, and most of all his unfailing wisdom. There was no question Solomon could not answer, and his poetry captured all the yearnings of the human heart.

But, like his father David, King Solomon was overcome by his own power. He married foreign women to forge political alliances, despite the Lord God's prohibition that Hebrews not marry foreigners, lest they be tempted to foreign gods. He had a thousand wives and concubines, and they turned his heart to lesser gods: Astarte, the naked fertility goddess, and the Ammonite god, Molech, whose worshipers placated his wrath by sacrificing children. As he had built a temple to the Lord, he now built a temple to Chemosh, god of the underworld. And he turned his people into slaves. No better than Pharaoh.

So the Lord was angry with Solomon, who had become no longer Solomon the Wise but Solomon the Magnificent. The Lord appeared to the self-absorbed old king and said, "Because you have broken your covenant with me, I will give your kingdom to one of your officials. Because you were once faithful, I will not do it in your lifetime. But your son will lose his crown, and ever after the kings of Israel will all be petty tyrants."

When Solomon began to repair the city walls, he appointed a young overseer named Jeroboam, and he was so impressed by his work he put him in charge of all the slaves. But the Lord came to Jeroboam and said, "You will be king when Solomon dies, and the kingdom shall be divided against itself, because Solomon in his arrogance has fled to other gods." When Solomon heard of that, he tried his best to kill Jeroboam, but he escaped to Egypt. And Jeroboam waited.

So Solomon died, and his son succeeded him. But not for long. The people said to the new king, "Your father treated us harshly. Lighten our burdens, and we will be loyal." But Solomon's son dismissed them and turned to the tyrannical ways of his father in his old age. So the people revolted, summoning Jeroboam from Egypt to be king of the north, leaving Solomon's son no more than a petty chieftain in Jerusalem. And slowly, the kingdom of

David and Solomon broke down and was swept away into the hands of invaders for the next three thousand years.

Male Archetypes in SOLOMON

	Archetype	Shadow	Balance
King	Responsibility for others	Tyranny	Concern for others

KING

Like "Patriarch," the word "King" isn't much appreciated in the Church today. Though Jesus used it himself, even the word "Kingdom" has too much of a proprietorial, male-dominating ring to it, and it has been softened to the gentler "Realm." But "Realm" has a too "settled and peaceful" tone to it, like a pleasant little countryside with the peasants cozy and at peace. On the contrary, the Kingdom Jesus describes is rather something toward which we are on the march, struggling to establish against great odds, a reality that has to be pursued aggressively.

Another negative spin to the word "King" comes from the fact we live in a democracy where kings became quite unpopular 200 years ago. It was okay for Princess Diana to come over every once in awhile, flash her perfect smile, and cuddle a few babies, but we were content when she got back on her jet and went back where royalty is more welcome. We don't like Bosses. But just as with "Patriarch," entirely rejecting the word "King" throws out a lot of good with the bad—and it surely denies that God is, in fact, the Boss, no matter how original sin resents that fact.

The King in a man takes charge; he feels responsible both to God and to his people. Like the young Solomon, he prays, and when he does he asks for "a heart to know right from wrong" *so that* he can serve both God and his people well. He is not a tyrant or a politico, but rather stands as a lens focusing the needs of the people to God and the will of God to the people.

A man of such selfless integrity at least does not seem to be the model of most leaders today. At best, a lawmaker seems loyal chiefly to the vested interests of his own constituents, trying to pork-barrel government concessions to them, not only because they elected him, but also in the hope they'll do it again. With such heavy dependence on the very expensive media to make the candidate known, and with the consequent dependence on big-bucks contributors (who have their own vested interests), it becomes difficult to say an elected official's primary interest is even in his constituents, much less the population of the country at large, much less to the truth.

The mark of the good King is compassionate responsibility, open-heartedness and openhandedness—all that Solomon lost when he grew successful and convinced himself all his achievements had come only through his own efforts alone (as the Magician-shadow believes his peculiar power derives from himself). When one has been gifted with talent, good family, good education, then *noblesse oblige:* The giftedness places the burden of sharing those gifts with the less gifted. As Jesus said, "From him to whom much has been given, much will be expected."

Probably few who read these pages will consider themselves extraordinarily gifted, though each of us—objectively—is. In the first place, none of us deserved even to be born. We didn't exist; how could we *deserve* anything? Granted, if we'd never been born, we'd never know the difference. But we *do* exist! Just try to list all the people you love, who enrich your life; list all the things you find precious—sunny days, swimming, music, playing football—uncountable. All of those things hinged on that one fundamental gift. Each of us was invited to this "party" without having merited an invitation. But another reason for our lack of gratitude is that we spend our (limited) time at the party looking not at the people who are less well off but at people who seem more unfairly gifted than we are. Therefore, envy replaces gratitude, and we go through life discontent—without comprehending that we never had any right to be here at all!

Who wouldn't be grateful? But it's difficult to feel grateful when you don't feel gifted. That's why Mass is called "The Eucharist." It means "thanksgiving." If Mass is boring, it might be that we're really too spoiled.

Beyond gratitude, another result of understanding our giftedness ought to be a sense of those people at the party who are *not* as gifted as we've been: the children of Appalachia and Angola, street people, babies with AIDS; the list is endless. Your time and resources are limited, so you can't reach out to all the varied needy, but if you are a man of honor, you have to choose just one group you *can* help. And a man's concern ought not to be limited to dramatic cases of need, far away. There are less gifted people right at your elbows who *deserve* your attention and respect: the people who clean up the cafeteria, check-out workers, sweeps, the person who asks for a handout on the street. Many fear, if they give change to a derelict, he or she will use the money for booze or drugs. But when you give a gift certificate, do you say, "Be sure to use that for something I'd approve of now"? Is it a gift or not? And what's the person asking? The cost of one phone call. The big question is not whether the beggar is honest but whether you are caring.

At first, Solomon was grateful for his gift of wisdom, and his gratitude turned him outward to the needs of his people. Then he began at least to act as if he had somehow bestowed his gifts on himself, and he turned more and more inward, losing his greatest gift: wisdom.

The shadow side of the King is really twofold: The King Run Wild at one extreme, the King Fallen Asleep at the other. When a man's talents are unchecked by loving concern for the people, he becomes the empty-hearted tyrant Solomon became in his old age; when he ignores loving concern entirely, his talents devolve into empty-headed, rootless childishness, like Sam Malone, the eternal adolescent. The King Run Wild shadow is not merely found in notorious cases, like Nero, Napoleon, Hitler, and Saddam Hussein. We also find it in all kinds of assistant managers, parking meter police, little men made suddenly "powerful" by a set of keys.

In the King Fallen Asleep, we find the responsibility and concern of the genuine King almost entirely dead in men of no commitment, all blow-dried hair and easy charm, men who make no difference, who nickel-and-dime their lives away on one self-indulgent kick after another.

In any school there are boys whose inner King has gone haywire, unchecked by any felt sense of the needs of others: the little-league Ayatollahs who throw their weight around—not only physically but with an arsenal of sly intimidations: the hotshots, the metalheads, the bikers, who walk around in cliquish cocoons and contribute nothing of themselves, who seem to absorb what pleases them without giving anything back. But there seem to be far more whose inner King has gone to sleep, or more likely died: the majority who allow themselves to be cowed, who never object, who never question—sheep.

Something can be done about the petty tyrants, the ones who make almost a career of detention. A boy who feels his inner King coming alive will swallow his fears and say to the self-absorbed peacocks, "Look. Will you *stop?*" But there's little one can hope to do to arouse the dormant inner King—or any emotion at all, other than resentment—in the willing sheep who want only to be unbothered. Too bad, really, because their punishment is to *be* perfectly dismissable.

Like the other archetypes, the inner King in a man is a potential waiting for a challenge, and the question to ask to determine if your own inner King is ready for the lightning stroke is: In your most honest mind, do you genuinely want to be a leader, or do you *say* you do but really prefer the security of being a follower? If you are in charge, will you be more interested in the profit-and-loss ledgers or in the people who work for you and the people you serve? Will you be the kind of man who gives bonuses, knows who's having a baby and send flowers, know who's bereaved and be at the funeral? Will you be the kind of man whose children believe he is usually right, because he's thought things out for himself, because he's wise?

The only way to answer those questions about the future is honestly to consider how you rise to the challenge right now. Don't be either too quick or too easy on yourself. "As grows the twig, so grows the tree." What concrete evidence have you from your consistent behavior now on which to ground the hope you will most likely be a leader and not a follower?

There was probably never a boy who didn't hope to be somebody some day, to change things, to show 'em all! The difference between those who do and those who don't is not a matter of native talent but of self-confidence—no matter what one's shortcomings. Everyone who ever became a somebody was once a nobody; every man who ever made a difference was once a boy. The key is resolve. The inner King will not come alive uninvited.

For further discussion see the appendix,
pages 182–183.

6 ELIJAH:
WILDMAN/HEALER

O nce upon a time, after the Hebrews had split into two
kingdoms, north and south, there came to the throne
of the northern kingdom a man named Ahab, arguably the
most detestable in a line of pretty unsavory Hebrew kings.
The Canaanites had become Hebrew subjects, just as the
Palestinians are in Israel today. But the Hebrews were poor
mountain folk, while the subject Canaanites cultivated the
rich plains, worshiping the fertility god, Baal, and were
richer even than their Hebrew kings.

This Baal seemed to know how to get things done, while
the Hebrew God seemed singularly silent. Perhaps more
persuasive: If a man had the choice between bowing in an
empty temple as a servant of Yahweh or engaging in rituals
involving temple prostitutes as a servant of Baal, a weaker
man's faith in Yahweh might suffer severe strain. Such it
was with Ahab. Not only did he marry a pagan, the
notorious Jezebel, but he built altars to the fertility god,
Baal, and worshiped him.

Around the country, holy men clad in ragged garments
roamed from camp to camp, exhorting the Hebrews to
remain faithful to the old ways, chief among them the
prophet Elijah, clad in animal skins cinched with a strap,
and not overly concerned about personal hygiene. Few

listened. Orgies were more enjoyable. So Elijah decided to attack the problem at its roots.

One day, out of nowhere, Elijah burst into the court of Ahab and Jezebel and shouted to the astonished audience: "In the name of the Lord I serve, I swear not a drop of rain will fall on this kingdom until I say so." And in a whirl of noxious odors, he was gone. A desolating drought fell on the land, and the Lord told Elijah to flee Ahab's wrath, into the wilderness on the far side of the Jordan, where a small stream still trickled, and the wildman Elijah was alone with Yahweh.

Then one day the Lord directed Elijah to leave the wilderness and go to the town of Zarephath where he would meet a widow who would care for him. As Elijah came to the town, he saw a woman gathering firewood and asked if she would feed him. "By the living God," she said, "with this drought, I have nothing but a handful of flour and a bit of olive oil. I'm gathering a few sticks to make a final meal for myself and my son. Then we will starve." But Elijah smiled, "Don't worry. Make us a small loaf. The Lord will never let the bowl run out of flour or the jar run out of oil until the rains come." So she did as he told her, and the three made bread from the flour and oil, day after day.

In the third year of the drought, the Lord sent Elijah back to Ahab. The king rose in fury. "You! The cause of this devastation!" But Elijah faced him down. "I'm not the cause," he cried. *"You* are, with your pagan idols. Summon your Baal priests and meet me on Mount Carmel. We will put it to the test. If the Lord is God, worship him. If Baal is God, worship him."

So Ahab was shamed into the trial between Yahweh and Baal, and he met Elijah on the mountain with not one but 450 Baal priests—just to be sure. "Bring two bulls," Elijah said. "Let your priests cut up one and put it on the wood, and I will do the same with the other. There are 450 of them and only one of me. We will see whose god has power.

Let the Baal priests pray to their god, and I will pray to mine. Whoever's god ignites the sacrifices, he is the only true God."

So the Baal priests danced around their altar, pleading with Baal to prove himself, but no fire came. Elijah laughed: "Pray louder!" he cried. "Perhaps your Baal's day-dreaming. Maybe off relieving himself? Off on a trip? Snoozing? Shout louder and wake the old cuss up!" They prayed louder, and hooted and howled, and cut themselves with knives. But no fire came.

Then Elijah stepped to the altar of the Lord. Three times he had the onlookers saturate the pieces of the bull and firewood with water, upping the odds against himself. Then he raised his arms over the sacrifice and prayed, "O Lord, God of Abraham, Isaac, and Jacob, prove now you are God and I am your servant." And in a whoosh, the altar was ablaze, crackling the meat, devouring the wood, and even cracking the stones beneath them. And the people shouted, "Yes! The Lord is our God!"

Elijah left the altars and climbed to the parched moun-taintop, and the Lord said, "Look west, toward the sea." But Elijah saw nothing. Seven times he climbed to the crest, and at last he said to the Lord, "I see nothing. Only . . . only a cloud no bigger than a fist! Ah!," he said to his servant, "run to Ahab. Tell him to climb into his chariot fast. He's going to be drenched!" The skies opened, and the land ran with water again. But Ahab, furious, ordered Elijah's death, so he fled once again, this time to the southern desert of Sinai, where Moses had met the Lord.

Alone in the barren desert, exhausted and starving, Elijah crawled into a cave and fell into a benumbed sleep. But suddenly he jerked awake. "Elijah," the voice of the Lord flashed. "What are you doing tombed in this cave?" But Elijah moaned, "Lord God! I've served you. Only you. But the people have broken covenant, torn down your altars, killed your prophets. I'm the only one left! And now they want to kill me!"

"Come out!" the Lord cried. But Elijah was weary and afraid. Outside, a furious wind arose, but Elijah clung to his womblike cave. Then the earth trembled, and he could feel the rock burn. Then silence. Then a still, small voice: "Elijah?" So Elijah crept from the cave and stood before the Lord. "Go back," the Lord said. "On your way, you will meet a young man named Elisha. Anoint him your successor as my prophet." So as he headed back to Samaria, Elijah met a young man plowing behind his oxen and he said, "Come. The Lord has need of you." And from that day, Elisha became Elijah's disciple.

Elijah found Ahab admiring the vineyard of a man Jezebel had ordered murdered in order to get it. Ahab saw him and said, "So. You've caught up with me, my enemy." But Elijah said, "You are your own enemy. You have murdered an innocent man and taken his property. Repent. If you don't, every male member of your family will die, and Jezebel's corpse will be gnawed to bits by every dog in the town." So, terrified of the Lord, Ahab repented. For awhile.

Wearily, sensing an ending to his trials, Elijah took Elisha on a journey to the banks of the River Jordan. As they stood above the muddy brown stream, Elijah turned to the young man and asked, "What do you want of me before I'm taken away?" And Elisha said, "If I'm to succeed you, give me your power." Elijah replied, "If you see me as I am taken, you will have my power."

Suddenly, miraculously, a chariot pulled by fiery horses appeared before them in a whirlwind of flame. "Father!" Elisha cried, as Elijah climbed into the chariot. And he watched as the steeds snorted flame and rose into the air, carrying Elijah away.

But at his feet lay Elijah's cloak, the mantle of his power.

Male Archetypes in *ELIJAH*

	Archetype	Shadow	Balance
Wildman	*Freedom and adaptability*	*"Wilding"*	*Service*
Healer	*Aggressive challenge of "illness"*	*Using spiritual power to harm*	*Emotional control*

WILDMAN

The archetype of the Wildman is not some kind of Charles Manson on a rampage. Rather, he is a man of nature: hunter, trapper, explorer, Indian scout, with a feel for the winds and rain, an easiness with wide-open spaces. He is the nomad sleeping in the souls of men since the days when we actually were roaming from encampment to encampment.

The process of civilization has been a process of "feminizing" the wildness out of the cavemen, the Vikings, the savage barbarians who came thundering into Europe and China in the Dark Ages. Civilization gave such lawless men a code, law, discipline. In the Middle Ages, the code of chivalry—all the things we associate with King Arthur and the Round Table—taught men to harness raw power in the service of justice, honor, protection of the exploited, especially women and children. In our own time, the women's movement has been admirably successful in convincing males that gentleness, empathy, and inclusiveness are as much qualities of a fulfilled male as they are of a fulfilled female.

But again, a man is not a woman. He loses something important in his psychological life when he eliminates his Wildman entirely. He becomes not merely civilized but tamed, domesticated, neutered. Chesterton says that, when the lion lies down with the lamb, we just assume the lion becomes lamblike. That, he says, is rank imperialism on the part of the lamb, the lamb devouring the lion instead of vice versa. Rather, the lion has to lie down with the lamb and still retain all his royal, leonine ferocity. It is not that a male must *become* the Wildman, but he must always remain *in touch* with his Wildman, or else he becomes nothing but a tame pussycat.

It is good for a man to have discipline, order, predictability. But also something within every man— something not entirely suspect—wants to shuck off our shirts and ties, bust free into the earthy, the carefree, the sloppy, to tell 'em all to go t'hell. It's the Crocodile Dundee in us.

But civilization—our society and our Church—doesn't want to let that surge of power loose. Business wants deodorized men in grey flannel uniforms and the latest designer neckties, presentable and predictable. This is a very serious enterprise, and we don't want anything wild-eyed or looney. In church, men should be as tame as children, while only a very few men (in dresses) lead them through their paces at Mass. There is no place for the exuberant, the enthusiastic, the carefree. (Perhaps that is one of the reasons rock concerts draw so many of us: They are a celebration of the Wildman, yearning to break free of the weeklong spiritual corsets.)

That suppression of the Wildman is also in direct contradiction to Jesus in the gospels: the Jesus who raged through the Temple with a whip driving out the moneymen, who stood fearlessly up to the officials of his own religion and called them hypocrites, vipers, and whitewashed tombs. To give credit to those who hanged Jesus, they didn't execute him because he turned the other cheek, remained predictably meek and mild, conformed like a sheep. They killed him because he refused to shut up.

The key to the Wildman is confidence, a healthy sense of self that—despite full awareness of his own shortcomings and weaknesses—refuses to be manipulated, degraded, or owned. Where does a man find that sense? It's highly unlikely he will find it in the uptight conformity of the office or the parish church or the lockstep day-to-day workings of a school. Elijah—and Moses and Jesus—found it in the wilderness, away from the distractions and intrusions of business, school, TV, newspapers, glaring lights, and blaring stereos. It is only out in the "desert," alone, that a man finds himself and God, understands both his vulnerability on the one hand and his stamina on the other. There he exchanges what he thought was real for the Really Real. The wilderness is a place of empowerment.

But most men—young or old—are too busy, too "tied up," to take time alone in retreat from the world. So they slog on, one day at a time, one-damn-thing-after-the-other, making a living, without any sense of what living is for.

The test of the authentic Wildman—as with all the other archetypes—is the purpose toward which his fierce power is directed: his own glorification or the service of others. Elijah uses his power for people: to feed the starving widow and her son, to call down fire and save the people from the drought. Why doesn't he—as so many modern men do— just mind his own business? Simply because he can't. He is driven, not by the need to succeed but by the need to help.

The major threat to the Wildman is burnout, when the need to see palpable results overshadows the mission, when the craving for concrete achievements outweighs the satisfaction of merely continuing to strive. Weary of apparently fruitless struggles to save the people from themselves, Elijah runs to the desert and enwombs himself in a cave. The death wish. This time the desert is not a place of empowerment but of escape. He is discouraged and fed up with people he's trying to help who consistently tell him just to get lost. Teachers know the feeling; so do police officers, social workers, health-care workers.

In the cave, Elijah succumbs to the death wish: the yearning just to be left alone. It's the overwhelming burden captured so dramatically in "Jesus Christ, Superstar," Jesus surrounded in a salt cave by lepers, pawing at him, groaning, and Jesus screams, "Leave me *alone!*" That event is not in the gospels, but if Jesus was totally, authentically human, he could hardly have avoided that discouragement, when nobody seemed to understand what he was doing, what he had come for, when all anyone wanted from his was a quick fix. Certainly he expresses it profoundly on the cross when he cries, "My God! My God! Why have you abandoned me?"

But God summons Elijah out of his womb-tomb, and at his bitterest moment, Jesus says, "Into your hands I commend my spirit." As with Peter walking on the water, if you can just keep your eyes on Jesus alone—and forget yourself, your bruised ego, your need for affirmation, you can do what you thought was impossible.

HEALER

To us, in our sophisticated, scientific world, the idea of the Priest-Magician seems embarrassingly primitive, believing that all sickness is rooted in the spirit. But for years doctors have known patients to have psychosomatic illnesses, genuine physical distress which has no discernible physical cause: rashes, ulcers, migraine headaches. These diseases are not caused by "demons" but by some confused kink in the soul, which has to be discovered and unraveled. Now more and more doctors also suspect that a healthy spirit—a positive, confident, faith-strengthened soul—can also help heal the body.

There is a difference between "masculine" healing and "feminine" healing (in both males and females). "Feminine" healing is nursing the patient, easing distress, soothing. "Masculine" healing is instead aggressive, combating the disease itself. That healing is often painful: cutting the flesh, drilling the tooth, forcing a victim of psychological problems to face the stinging truth. But without it, the victim goes on suffering. The most fortunate patients are those who have doctors and nurses (of no matter what sex) who have a healthy combination of both: both the knowledge and determination to uproot the causes of the illness but also the sensitivity to regard the patients as not merely biological problems but fellow human beings in misery.

For that reason, the best Healer has gone through his own harrowing: the wounded Healer whose knowledge—and acceptance—of his own weakness have *empowered* him, as the Wildman's sojourn in the wilderness empowers him with a sense both of his vulnerability but also his resourcefulness. Wounded Healers are the men who serve in Twelve-Step programs for recovering alcoholics and drug-abusers, who have themselves humbly admitted, "I just can't do it alone." Thus the victims are themselves ironically empowered by such men's accepted weakness.

Christian healing is available to all, no matter what their rank or lack of it, no matter how appealing or appalling the victim is, no matter how utterly "undeserving" the victim is. Jesus pointed that out with the Good Samaritan. If you read the story from the point of view of ordinary Jewish layfolk hearing it for the first time, your expectations of the story would be completely short-circuited—as Jesus consistently did.

The first potential source of help for the man in the ditch is a priest, but he averts his gaze and passes by. The second hope arrives in a Levite (the equivalent of a deacon), but no, he goes on his way, too. Now, after a priest, then a half-priest/half-layman, whom would you expect to be the third? Well, an ordinary Jewish layman, of course. But no! Not even a Jew, but a renegade Samaritan no Jew would want to be touched by. To understand the amazement of Jesus' audience at that outcome, imagine the victim in the ditch was the Grand Dragon of the KKK and the one who helped him was a black man. Or vice versa.

Probably more than a few reading this book have entertained the possibility of going into one of the healing professions: medicine, biological research, psychiatry, psychology, social service, priesthood—even politics could be used to effect healing. But that, of course, is a long way off. What about now? Not all suffering is physical. There are young men and women at your very elbows who need your creative concern, your time, perhaps even your forgiveness.

Within the first month or two of ninth grade, you can tell which boys were the first ones hit in the grade school dodgeball game, right? You may not have been responsible for his being so shy and fearful, but if your Healer is to awaken, you have to feel some kind of responsibility for helping him overcome those soul scars. There are boys in every gym class who couldn't get a basketball through the hoop if they were standing on Patrick Ewing's shoulders. You could help one. Just one. "Hey, wanna throw a few hoops? Just the two of us?" And then, without being obvious, give him a few pointers: "It works better for me if I hold the ball like this."

A very wise senior asked me a very perceptive question one time: "Why is fulfillment always in the future?" It doesn't have to be. There's need for healing all around us, and the thrill of making even the slightest difference in a wounded person's soul is the best kind of fulfillment there is. There's no lack of need. What's lacking is the self-confidence to say, "Maybe I can't make a big difference. But I want to try. Now."

For further discussion see the appendix,
pages 184–185.

7 JEREMIAH:
PROPHET

Once upon a time, during the reign of the Egyptian puppet king Zedekiah, there was a quite unpromising lad named Jeremiah. He was not just a kid, but spindly, and nothing-faced, nerdy, and he also had a pretty embarrassing stammer. By this time, knowing what a pushover the Lord is for nobodies, this Jeremiah wimp is in for the surprise of his life, right? Right you are.

There little Jeremiah was, minding his own business, when he was suddenly overwhelmed by a vision of God. The Lord said, "I chose you before you were born as a prophet to speak to all the nations." And Jeremiah stammered, "Sov-sov-sovereign Lord. I . . . I don't know how to speak. I am too young." But the Lord said, "Don't say you are too young! Go to the people and tell them what I want you to say. Don't be afraid of them. I'll be there to protect you." Then the Lord reached out and touched Jeremiah's rabbity lips and said, "There. I have given you the words. I will give you power to uproot nations. Look deeply into your heart. What do you see?" And Jeremiah said, "I see a great cauldron in the north, about to tip over!" And the Lord said, "Yes, I am calling the kings of the north to swarm over this faithless people who have gone over to the pagan gods. Go to this people and tell them that. They won't believe you. But don't be afraid. I will make you strong as a wall of brass."

So, terrified, young Jeremiah began to go from place to place in Jerusalem, trying to get the people to listen: "The Lord told me to proclaim this message. 'You were once a faithful people,' the Lord says. 'I committed myself to you as to my only wife. What have I done to you that you turned away to worthless idols? I led you from Egypt and gave you this land, and you've ruined it! Even my own priests care more for their own comforts than for me. You are no wiser than camels in heat. Whores! You murdered the prophets I sent to warn you. Well, now your own evil ways will punish you. Hah! Then turn to your pagan idols and beg them to save you. I divorce Israel, the jeweled, drunken whore. But . . . if only you will come back, I will take you back. If not, the enemies are just waiting to fall on you. They are coming! Mind you, they are already on their way!'"

Day after day, Jeremiah stood at the gates of the Temple, shouting to the people, "Change your ways. Stop taking advantage of alien people who look different from us! Take care of the homeless who lie in our streets! Stop ravaging our land and worshiping money! The Lord's Temple is not a hideaway for people with larcenous hearts! You've taken the wrong road. The only answer is to go back and start over! But you don't even ask where you're headed. You just rush headlong from one pleasure to the next. And even the Lord's priests say, 'That's just fine. Have you given your offering this week?' The Lord is going to throw you out of this land of promise. There is a great nation in the north that will turn Jerusalem into a desert!"

But anyone who troubled to listen merely sneered at little Jeremiah: "We are doing just fine. Go shout somewhere else." But there were some who were unnerved by what he said, fearful that, if they ever took Jeremiah seriously, they might have to change their pleasurable ways. So a group began to discuss ways to eliminate him. Even his own family would have nothing to do with him. And Jeremiah became sick with discouragement.

"God damn the day I was born!" he cried to the Lord. "You've cursed me to quarrel and argue with everyone in the land. It's for *your* sake I'm insulted. I'm drowning in anger." But the Lord said to him, "Go down to the potter's house and watch him work. He will be my answer to you." So Jeremiah watched the potter working his wheel, and whenever the piece of pottery was imperfect, the potter smashed the clay back on the wheel and made it into another pot entirely. "See?" said the Lord. "Don't I have the right to do with you what the potter does to his clay?" So Jeremiah relented, with a sigh. "A man does not make his God," he said, "God makes a man as God wills." And he went back to his endless preaching and bickering, and to the unrelenting dismissive sneers of his fellow Israelites. He went for years.

Pashur, the chief priest of the Temple, finally could take no more. He sent the Temple guards to seize Jeremiah, and they chained him to the Benjamin Gate of the Temple where every passerby could mock at him. Jeremiah was heartsick with rage at what the Lord had brought him to. "Lord," he cried, "you've deceived me! You don't play fair! You're stronger than I am. Everyone makes fun of me because of you! But when I tell myself to forget you and never speak your name again, your message keeps boiling up inside me. Curse the man who told my father, 'You have a son!' Was I born only to be a disgrace?"

But after 23 years of sneers and shame, Jeremiah's predictions began to take shape like a storm cloud. From the north came the legions of King Nebuchadnezzar of Babylon, gobbling up the country like ravenous wolves. And at last they were at the very gates of Jerusalem. The High Priest Pashur came to Jeremiah under orders from King Zedekiah. "Pray to the Lord for us," he pleaded. But the Lord told Jeremiah, "I am against them. They had the choice of the way that leads to life and the way that leads to death. And they have chosen the way that leads to death. They are a burden I can well live without. They will be given over to the King of Babylon."

Jeremiah tried to leave the city in fear of his life. But when he reached the Benjamin Gate, the officer in charge stopped him. "You're running to your Babylonians," he said. "That isn't so," Jeremiah pleaded. But the officer wouldn't listen and arrested him on the spot. They beat him and threw him first into an underground dungeon, then into a dry well. City officials were demanding Jeremiah's death, because his predictions were making the soldiers on the walls lose courage.

But King Zedekiah had Jeremiah brought to him and said, "I want you to tell me the whole truth." But Jeremiah replied, "If I tell you the truth, you will kill me. Your only hope is to surrender to King Nebuchadnezzar." But Zedekiah refused and thereby sealed his own doom and the doom of all his people.

The Babylonian hosts surrounded Jerusalem and finally broached its walls. By the thousands they came boiling into the city, slaughtering the guards and subduing all the people. King Zedekiah and his officials tried to escape the city by night, creeping out through the palace garden. But enemy soldiers captured him and took him to Nebuchadnezzar. As King Zedekiah looked on, his sons were executed along with all the royal officials. Then the invader king had Zedekiah's eyes torn from their sockets so the last thing he would ever see would be the gory corpses of his children. He was led off in chains to exile in Babylonia.

Meanwhile, the Babylonians burned down the Temple and the royal palace and set about tearing down the walls of Jerusalem. Nebuchadnezzar's men stripped the Temple of all its bronze and carried off anything made of gold or silver. Every able-bodied craftsman, his wife, and their

children, and all the Temple priests were bound in chains—
4,600 people, and the long line began out of the ruined
gates on the long trek to slavery in Babylonia.
Nebuchadnezzar decreed that all the land be turned over
to the landless peasants. And for 50 years, the cream of
Hebrew citizens would be slaves, far from home.

Male Archetypes in JEREMIAH

	Archetype	Shadow	Balance
Prophet	*Devotion to the truth*	*Self-pity; burn-out*	*Confidence in God*

PROPHET

The Prophet is the sleeping idealist in a man. To all the
other archetypes, he adds the element of fearless
confrontation: indicting, exhorting, challenging others to
stop kidding themselves and be what they were born to be.

The common use of the word "prophet" confines it to
one who predicts the future, and that is at least part of his
purpose. But the Greek root of the word is *pro-phemi*, "one
who speaks in someone else's place," in this case, for God.
Jeremiah was a prophet in both those senses: He saw which
way the wind was blowing. Violate the natures God
programmed into things and people, and sooner or later
those natures will rise up and take their revenge.

There's no getting away from it: Prophets are
obnoxious, not only to the people they're exhorting to
change their ways but often even to people who care for
them: "A martyr is somebody who lives with a saint."
Probably none of the archetypes is more susceptible to its
shadow side than the Prophet: the frustrated idealist who
devolves into the constant crank, the crotchety griper, the
yakkety-yak-yakking voice.

The real Prophet is a man of tough love. He has no illusions, especially not about himself or about his chances of changing the world dramatically. But he's by God going to try, simply because he couldn't sleep if he didn't. We all have our pet peeves, things that just simply shouldn't be that way: the unfair teacher, the john doors off the hinges for years, the guys who cut into the line. But most of us grit our teeth; grin and bear it. Not the Prophet.

The true Prophet keenly feels the struggle between good and evil, and while whatever changes he can cause will be minimal at best, he feels obligated to leave the world at least the tiniest bit *less* evil than when he found it. His confidence comes not from any exaggerated sense of himself but from the ideal he believes in and the cause he serves. The best of prophets are exceptionally realistic and tolerant, even of themselves. But they're more aware of the consequences of human choices than most allow themselves to be. You can buy on credit, skate on thin ice, play the odds, but not forever. And they have a *passion* to keep people from hurting themselves by their own choice.

Teachers often suffer the frustrations of the Prophet. Day after day, they keep exhorting young people to take hold of their learning rather than just doing the minimum for a diploma which is, in the end, false testimony to an education. Year after year, I say, "I have a crees-tal ball, and in the crees-tal ball I see dees boys next yhear. And de're saying, 'Damn! Hiff HI'd honely learnt to *write!*'" And year after year, they come back and say, "Ya know. You were right." Yep. I knew I was right. But they wouldn't believe me till it was too late. Now it will cost them $20,000 to learn how to write, and a great many of their college classmates are far and away ahead of them.

There is one very pointed statement in the Jeremiah story that you shouldn't overlook too self-defensively. Jeremiah offers what at first seems a legitimate alibi. He stammers, "I'm just a boy!" But the Lord says, "Don't *say*

I'm just a boy!" Of the thousands of young men I've taught, perhaps the majority have tried to argue out of both sides of their mouths: "Hey, I'm an adult. I can drive at night. I can drink." But when you ask, "When are you going to start going after your education the same way you expect your Dad to do his job?" the answer is almost invariably, "Hey, wait a minute! I'm only a *kid!*"

Nope, from the moment you passed puberty and were capable of fathering a child, you no longer have the right to that cop-out. You may not be psychologically ready to be a father yet, but you're sure not a kid anymore. That tag "-escence" on the word "adolescence" signifies a process that has begun but isn't yet finished, as in "convalescence." It's a *process*, just as infancy is. Every day, parents have to lure a baby into taking just a few steps more, throwing just a bit further, entertaining themselves just a touch longer (so Mommy can crash for awhile).

The same is true of adolescence. It's not some moratorium one drops into at puberty and doesn't emerge from until college graduation, during which time you do the minimum input for the maximum return. Every day, parents and teachers have to lure you to take on just a bit more adult responsibility for your own choices. If you've got a teacher who gives you even a D for ten minutes of swamp-gas essay, you've got a bad teacher, and you're throwing away good money—and a good mind—just to learn how to beat the system, which you learned back in grade school.

Don't say, "I'm just a boy." You haven't the right to.

At least in your best moments, you probably do have the itch to make a difference, to be somebody, to have your life amount to more than "the usual": dependable job, dependable wife, dependable kids, with no greater problems than getting rid of your crabgrass and cleaning your pool filter. Is that all there is?

There are plenty of people right at your elbows in need of your healing; there are plenty of things wrong with our common life that you could help change—not dramatically perhaps, but make a difference, even now. Edmund Burke said, "All that's needed for the triumph of evil is that good men be silent." You can't crusade for everything, but if you call yourself a man, you've by God got to crusade for something.

There's plenty to pick from. Our highways are full of litter; could you organize a project to pick up a section of freeway—and get the newspapers to cover it so people might be tempted to stop littering? Paint over a section of graffitied wall, even if you have to do it over and over again? There are plenty of homeless people huddled for warmth on the grates of our cities; could you and a few friends, once a month, pack a bag of sandwiches and hand them out? Every year I ask students to write an essay on something in the city that really ticks them off; then I hand out envelopes and ask them to address them to *The Daily News*. Groans worthy of Job: "What good would it do?" But we've all heard some politician say, "You know, I got a letter from a little girl out in Iowa the other day . . ."

The point is not the changes you can see as a result of your efforts. The point is the change in yourself.

As with Elijah, the problem for Jeremiah was burnout, self-pity. The shadow side of the prophet overwhelms his main asset: confident idealism. The curse of the Prophet is perfectionism, and his salvation is lowering his expectations down to nothing, so that every slightest success is an occasion for celebrating!

But there are times when all of us feel God has betrayed our trust. Even when we know God's ways are not our ways, that our minds are too small to encompass God's reasons, we still feel let down. At those times, it is not only wise but healthy to do precisely what Jeremiah did: Take God for a walk and bawl hell out of him—then forgive God, for all the good times, which have certainly outnumbered the bad.

There's no problem with having a dust-up with God; the patriarch Jacob did just that, and his name was changed to Israel: "He who wrestles with God." But we can't *control* God. God is not ours; we are his. God's lesson to Jeremiah was a visit to the potter: If God's not satisfied with the extent to which we've grown, God throws us back on the wheel and fashions us into something better. God has some unreadable reason for cancer and AIDS, hurricanes and drought, suffering innocents. If he doesn't, life is insupportable and absurd. We have to forgive God for having reasons God can't share, just as we have to forgive teachers for knowing more than we do.

Ask your inner prophet: Do you really believe people can be changed—not everybody, not even any individual all at once, but at least bit by bit? More important, do you honestly believe *you* ought to try to help them, challenge them, "invite them higher"? When a friend—or family member—is hurting himself or herself and others, do you have to courage to call them on it?

The true Prophet knows the difference between optimism and hope. Optimism doesn't see the costs; it's the student who knows "it's a jungle out there," yet is unshakably convinced he's gonna show 'em all, even if he does no real learning at all! Hope knows the road is rocky and filled with washouts and crawling with ogres and dragons, but says, "Why not? It's worth a try, right? Who knows? Let's give it a shot."

And don't say, "I'm just a boy."

For further discussion see the appendix, pages 186–187.

8 JONAH:
TRICKSTER

Once upon a time there was a young man named Jonah who made it a point to keep his nose clean, mind his own business, and generally avoid the spotlight. But as we've seen, the Lord God has a marked aversion to complacency. So one day the voice of God begins to echo in Jonah's brain: "Go to the great city of Nineveh in Assyria and speak out against it. I want you to convert them. If not, in 40 days I'll blast 'em t'hell."

Jonah shook his head. "I must be coming down with something," he said, and tried to keep himself occupied. But the voice persisted: "Go to the great city of Nineveh in Assyria and speak out against it. . . ." Jonah said to himself, "That's perfectly ridiculous! Nineveh? In the first place, it's 500 miles away. I'd wear my legs down to stumps. In the second place, they're not just foreigners but *pagans!* In fact, the word 'pagan' doesn't even cover it. Nineveh's a swamp of lust, greed, corruption, and filth. Not to mention sin. An *army* of prophets couldn't convert Nineveh. Not in a century. And *I'm* going to convert them, by *myself?* That's the craziest idea I ever heard. Besides, in the third place, the Lord is a merciful God. Would the Lord destroy a city when there must be at least a *few* innocents there? Of course not. Not the Lord." But the voice of the Lord persisted: "Go to the great city of Nineveh. . . ."

So Jonah, being practical, decided it was time for a long, well-earned vacation. He closed up his shop and, though Hebrews were terrified of the sea, hightailed it to the port of Joppa and secured passage on a ship bound to Spain—which was about as far from that Nineveh as you could get. If Nineveh was to the east, then westward ho! But even though his nerves were knots of barbed wire, the voice in his head kept whispering: "Go to the great city of Nineveh. . . ."

When the Lord sets his mind to something, the cards are stacked. No sooner had the ship gotten out into deep waters but the Lord raised up a typhoon like none any sailor had ever seen. Sails shredded, masts cracked, and the crew was terrified. They threw the cargo overboard. They screamed prayers into the teeth of the gale, each in his own language to his own god. Finally, the captain went below and found Jonah, sleeping like a child in the midst of chaos. "Get up," he shouted. "Pray to *your* god. Maybe *he'll* feel sorry for us." Jonah tried, but no prayer on earth could battle that insistent voice in his head.

Finally, the sailors cast lots to find who was the cause of this fury of the gods, and of course Jonah's name was picked. Every eye riveted on him through the slashing rain. "Where are you from? What are you doing here?" And Jonah said, "My name is Jonah, which means 'pigeon,' which is precisely what I am. I'm a Hebrew. I'm running away from this voice in my head. My God seems to be asking me to convert Nineveh. Nineveh! Now isn't that silly?" The sailors were furious. "How dare you avoid a call from your god? Well, what are we supposed to do to calm this storm?" Jonah sighed, aware of the inevitable. "Throw me overboard," he said. "It's me the Lord's after. The sea will calm down." So without a second's delay, the sailors followed Jonah's excellent advice and chucked him into the sea. And the sea went suddenly calm, slick as slate.

But the Lord, in control as usual, had a huge fish just waiting to gobble up Jonah, and the fish nosed back east in the direction of Joppa—and Nineveh. For three days, sloshing around inside the fish's belly with half-digested sea bass and clots of kelp, Jonah had plenty of time to think—and pray. "O Lord, you've brought me to the dark depths. Save me, and I will sing your praises forever!" And with a loud "Ka-pooey!" the fish spat Jonah up onto the beach at Joppa.

So Jonah slogged his way along the 500 miles to Nineveh, a city so large it took three days to walk through it. He trudged its streets, crowded with vendors and buyers and prostitutes, shouting, "In 40 days, Nineveh will be blasted t'hell!" People stopped dead in their tracks, faces sagging, wondering if this was a prophet or a paranoid, because just about everybody in town over the age of five had reason for a guilty conscience.

When the king—who had more on his conscience than most—heard about this strange warning, he sent out a proclamation, just in case this looney was on the level. No one was to eat anything. They were to wear nothing but burlap. Everyone was to pray earnestly to this Lord to change his mind. And God saw and, indeed, did change his mind and refused to punish them.

Meanwhile, Jonah had climbed a high hill outside the city to watch the great show when fire and brimstone rained down on Nineveh. And he waited. It wasn't possible. It had worked! Which didn't please Jonah one bit. "Lord," he grumped, deprived as he was of the expected spectacle, "didn't I say when I left home that this is just what you'd do? Didn't I say, 'The Lord is a loving and merciful God? He'd never destroy that city.' Isn't that what I said?" But the Lord said, "What right have you to be angry?" But Jonah, shamed that he'd been used as a dupe for a plan the Lord had no intention of carrying out anyway, went out in the sun, half hoping he'd die of heat prostration.

But the Lord raised up a huge castor-oil plant by Jonah's side and sent a cool breeze, and Jonah sat comfortably in the cool shade and did what he did best: He fell asleep. But the Lord sent a worm into the plant while Jonah slept, and the plant went limp and quickly died. As the sun rose, the Lord sent a stifling east wind from the desert, and Jonah woke choking for breath. "So," he snarled, "you led me this whole merry dance from my home, to the middle of the sea, through this godforsaken wilderness, through that wretched city shouting like a fool, only to fry me to death out here? That plant was saving my life in this furnace, and you killed it." But the Lord said, "What right have you to be angry?" Jonah crossed his arms and hunched his shoulders and sat there grumping in the searing sunlight. "I have *every* right to be angry," he said. "Angry enough to die."

The Lord said, "The plant that protected you grew up in one night and disappeared the next day. You didn't make it grow. I took pity on you, didn't I? How much more should I pity the hundred thousand innocent children of Nineveh? Go home now. You've served me well. You deserve a rest."

So Jonah rose and began his long journey home, suspecting that—the Lord being the Lord—his rest wouldn't last very long.

Male Archetypes in JONAH

	Archetype	Shadow	Balance
Trickster	*Exuberant fun*	*Terminal adolescence*	*Meditation; a schedule*

TRICKSTER

The Trickster has been an archetype in all literature, from Homer's mischievous Hermes to Shakespeare's wise fools.

In the Uncle Remus stories, Br'er Rabbit outfoxes Br'er Fox—and quite often himself. In our own day, Hobbes lies in wait to pounce on Calvin, the Roadrunner beep-beeps by Wile E. Coyote, Hawkeye Pierce and B.J. Hunnicutt conspire against everyone in the 4077, and sometimes get blown up by their own bombs.

If we are to avoid the iron pomposity of Puritanism, we need the Trickster to keep us laughing at ourselves, to force us to make peace with the hidden, shadow parts of our souls. Even (perhaps especially) the Church and church-folk need the sly distorting mirrors of Fr. Guido Sarducci and the Church Lady.

In scripture, God himself is often the Trickster, and the story of Jonah's attempts to escape the will of God are as laughable as Roger Rabbit's trying to outwit Baby Herman. His very name means "pigeon," gull, dupe. Try as he might to elude God, God always wins. As we have seen in several stories before, we have a certain sympathy with his alibis; in fact, we often take refuge in the same ones ourselves: "I stammer! I'm only a boy! Nineveh? Are you out of your mind?" It's like Obiwan Kenobi coming to young Luke Skywalker and saying, "Right, now! Let's go out and take on the whole Evil Empire!" Sure.

It's worth noting that throughout the Old Testament, the prophets are notoriously windy. The prophet Jeremiah, for instance, goes on and on for 50-plus chapters, over and over the same woeful predictions. And for all his wind, it doesn't work. Not a single prophet in all the Hebrew Scriptures got anybody to change, at least not for long. Except Jonah!

He just says one sentence, "In 40 days Nineveh will be blasted t'hell." And it works! For the first and only time in the entire Bible! (Which might give homilists food for thought about shortening their sermons.)

And is Jonah steamed! He knew it all along; God wouldn't be that vindictive. So why did God send him on a fool's errand back and forth from one end of the world to the other? What's more, he was waiting for a spectacular show and it didn't materialize. Jonah forgets that he was the instrument God used to save all those people from themselves. So he grumps. And while he sulks, God teases him again, lulling him to sleep under the castor-oil plant, then pulling the rug out from under him again. And the clue to Jonah's anger at God is that Jonah thought he had some rights where God was concerned. There's a crucial insight there which even most adults balk at.

Whenever somebody asks me, "How ya doin'?" I always answer, "Better than I deserve!" Almost always, they look at me puzzled. Some say, "Oh, of course you deserve *some*thing." But I don't. I didn't deserve to be born. My mother and father could have practiced birth control or had an abortion; God could have been too busy at the time for one more little redhead. I didn't exist; how could a non-existent have deserved anything? Everything that I hold precious depended on that first, unmerited gift of existence. Therefore, everything I have and everything that happens to me is a gift, even the crap. "Better than I deserve!"

But we take existence for granted, just as we do a long and fortunate life. But as Chesterton said, if Cinderella goes to the Fairy Godmother and complains about having to leave the ball early, the Godmother had every right to retort, "Who said you could go to the ball in the first place?" It's understandable that people grieve for awhile at the loss of a loved one, but a great many never realize they could never have known that person at all; even for the short time they knew that person, he or she was a gift. A good many people spend their lives griping their accommodations at the ball: "They're better situated than I am; His clothes are better than mine; He got a better body . . ." and on and on. Never once pausing to reflect on the fact they did nothing to be invited to the ball in the first place.

Job went through the same agony, arguing with his friends for 40 chapters about why God would allow him to suffer so. Surely anyone suffering as intolerably as he was would at least *remember* what incredible wickedness he had committed to deserve such extreme agony. But when God finally arrives (in a whirlwind—which isn't playing "fair" either!), God doesn't give an answer. Instead, he asks Job a series of questions, beginning with, "Where were you when I laid the foundations of the earth? . . . Should I check my plans with you?"

We forget we are answerable to God, not the other way round. Our minds are simply too small to encompass God's mind. Job gets no answer to his questions about his guilt, simply because he was asking the wrong questions. The real question was: Who is God, and who am I in relation to God? When Job meets God and *really* sees who God is, his questions cease. God doesn't *give* the answer; God *is* the answer.

One of the greatest men I've ever met was a merchant marine veteran in a terminal cancer hospital. He'd lost his larynx and could communicate only in writing. He'd also contracted tuberculosis and was in isolation. One Saturday, I said, "Bill, it must get very lonely," and he wrote on his pad with a shining smile, "Yes, but isn't it wonderful God trusts me enough to give it to me?" That's the genuine article.

The greatest "trick" God plays on us is simply being God, someone that we—no matter what our IQs or how many degrees we have—simply can't comprehend.

Throughout the Scriptures God plays the Trickster, invariably short-circuiting our expectations. If one of us were looking for a couple to be the grandparents of uncountable Hebrews, of course the first couple we'd ask would be Abram and Sarai, barren as a pair of bricks. If we wanted a charismatic leader to bring the Hebrews out of Egypt, the first man who'd come to mind would be Moses, a stammering coward who tried every weaseling trick in the book to get out of it. If the task were to bring down Goliath, of course we'd go to a family of Arnold Schwartzenegger brothers and say, "Oh, no. I'd prefer that spindly kid from the sheepfold, the one with the slingshot, please." If we were looking for the mother of the Messiah, we'd obviously bypass Rome, Alexandria, Athens, and head straight for a no-name village in a no-name province and ask the *permission* of a hill country girl. If the search were on for the leader of a worldwide campaign—one to sell something as unappetizing as taking up a cross, daily—who'd spring to mind quicker than Peter, who misunderstood the whole purpose of the campaign, consistently, who denied even knowing you—not once, but three times, with plenty of time between to realize what he was doing, and not to a soldier with a knife at his throat but to a *waitress!* God's ways are not our ways, and that's the truth.

There's a pattern there.

God is faithful, but God's sure not predictable! Like Jonah, all we want is to be left alone, to find some security, to sleep. But God isn't into *thanatos;* he's very much into *eros:* life. Apparently, God likes good stories, and stories are deadly dull without unexpected curves in the road, unkindly ogres, fire-breathing dragons. Oh, you can more or less avoid having an interesting life, simply by ignoring God's calls or, like Jonah, running as fast as you can in the other direction: to wall-to-wall music God can't penetrate, to fast cars that give you the illusion of making progress without effort, to easy sex which is in the end more an anesthetic than a stimulant. But you'll be the walking punishment of your own evasions: empty, dull, unmemorable. When you play with God, the cards are stacked.

If we're to pattern our lives on God, then we need not only God's King, God's Prophet, God's Magician; we also need God's Trickster. The healthy Trickster who can avoid being merely a hemorrhoidal practical joker is a good friend who shakes us up when we're wallowing in self-pity. Without him, we convince ourselves our problems really are earth-shattering (because we act as if we, not God, are the focus of reality). When we swell up with our own self-importance, we're fortunate if a gentle Trickster sneaks up behind us and bursts our silly balloon.

Pope John XXIII was an unexpected Trickster. After the long reign of the patrician, unsmiling, ramrod-straight Pius XII, who bounces out on that balcony but a fat little peasant with a sweet-potato nose and Dumbo ears, beaming. And since the tailors had never expected any cardinal that short and fat to be chosen, they had to jerryrig a white cassock so tight the little man couldn't raise up his arms, so he gave his first blessing "from the hip" like a penguin trying to fly! He was unselfconscious, down-to-earth, making little jokes, especially on himself. When asked how many people worked in the Vatican, he replied, "About half." When he saw the first Vatican stamps bearing his picture, he moaned, "God knew for 77 years I'd become pope. Couldn't he have made me more photogenic?" When former president Eisenhower visited, John apologized for his poor English: "They're trying to teach me, but I'm the lowest one in the class."

And he was unpredictable! A month after his election, just after the Christmas Mass, off he went without warning anyone to the children's hospitals in Rome. The following day, he was in the maximum security section of Rome's largest prison, confessing he'd once stolen an apple, but they couldn't convict him because he'd eaten the evidence. And within three months of his election, in an announcement that sent a shockwave through the whole Church, he announced the convening of Vatican II.

Ask your inner trickster: Do you take yourself too seriously, as if the whole world were on your shoulders? Have you the good sense to laugh at yourself? When you really make a serious mistake—or perhaps even sin—do you have the good grace to confess it and apologize, trusting you'll be forgiven and it will all be forgotten? Or on the other hand, is your Trickster too often out of control? Can you harness him with a schedule?

It's quite possible you could lead a reasonably satisfying life in security, making no waves, arousing no criticism, being generally unbothered. But except for perhaps your children, you will not really have made much difference, will you?

And you will have run away from God.

For further discussion see the appendix,
pages 187–189.

9 JESUS:

All the Archetypes in One

O nce upon a time there was this wealthy farmer. Call him Eli. He had two sons. Reuben, the eldest, was like the ant in Aesop's story: hardworking, predictable, and as lively as stale bread; the younger, Joseph, was like Aesop's grasshopper: sprightly, carefree, and (though Eli would never admit it) his father's pet.

One day, out of the blue, Joseph came to Eli and said, "Father, I feel stifled here. I need elbow room. Would you give me my half of our inheritance now, while I'm still young enough to enjoy it?" And without a word or a question, Eli divided his property with his two sons. Reuben and Joseph went to the bankers, where Reuben deposited his share and Joseph turned it into cash.

Off Joseph went to the city of Nineveh, where pleasure ruled (for anyone with cash) and the women were beyond scruples or surprise. But within a few weeks of wild carousing, Joseph had frittered away half of what his father had worked a lifetime for. Worse, a terrible famine stalked the country like a ravenous wolf, and the only work Joseph could find was feeding bean pods to pigs, which to a Jew were as repellent as lepers. His belly groaned with hunger, but he feared that, if he filched food from the pigs, he'd be sent away.

One cold dark night, crying himself to sleep, he suddenly sat up. "How many of my father's hired workers have more than enough to eat, and here I am devoured by hunger!" Scrubbing the tears from his cheeks, he stood up and grabbed for his staff. "I will go to my father and say, 'Father, I've sinned against God and against you. I'm not fit anymore to be called your son. But treat me like one of your hired men.'" So he set off on the long journey home.

While Joseph was still a long way off, Eli saw him, and his old heart welled up with pity and joy. He hiked up his skirts and ran down the hill, out through the rolling fields toward the haggard boy trudging the road. Eli threw his arms around Joseph's shoulders and hugged him hard, weeping and laughing at once, kissing his son's cheeks again and again.

Joseph pulled away, his head hanging, his body bent in shame. "Father," he began the speech he had been repeating in his head for endless miles, "I have sinned against God and against you. I am no longer fit to be called. . . ."

"My son!" Eli cried, raising his arms to heaven, and turning up toward the house. "Quick!" he cried. "One of you bring the best robe for him. And a ring. And his feet are bloody and bound in rags. Bring sandals! Get that prize calf and kill it. We shall have a *feast!*" he shouted. "My son who was dead is *alive* again! *Alive!*"

And so the feasting began. But Reuben, who had been working in one of the farthest fields, was just bringing his crew of men back when he heard the sound of music and dancing coming from the house. While he washed at the trough, he called a servant. "What's all this noise?" he asked. The servant grinned, "Joseph has come home! So your father killed the prize calf because he's back safe and sound."

Reuben hurled his staff in a rage and stalked away, trembling with fury. This was *his* farm now, *his* house, *his* prize calf. But the servant had told Eli of Reuben's anger, and the old man came out to him, begging him to come inside. "Look, father," Reuben said through his gritted teeth, "all these years I've slaved for you. I *never* complained. I *never* disobeyed. And did you ever say, 'Thanks, Reuben, you're a fine son"? Did you ever give *me* even a ropey old *goat* to party with my friends? No! But this ungrateful son of yours goes off, wastes half of what you've worked your life for with whores, and when he drags his sorry ass back you give him the prize calf to celebrate . . . what? Because we got this leech, this loser *back?*"

Eli looked sadly at his older boy. "Reuben," he said, tears rimming his eyes, "you are my son. You are always with me, and all that I have is yours. But couldn't you open your heart? We *had* to celebrate and be happy. Joseph was dead, and now he's *alive!* He was lost, and now he's come *home!*"

Reuben turned, scowling, and walked away.

THE PRODIGAL FATHER

If all the copies of the gospels in the world somehow disappeared, and only the story we call "The Prodigal Son" remained, I think we could clone out the entire gospel message from it.

First of all, the story is misnamed. "Prodigal" means squandering, wasteful, incautious, and those words surely describe the younger son. But the *father* is the only one in both halves of the story, and he is the one I suspect Jesus wants us to identify with. The father—like God—is truly prodigal, squandering, wasteful, incautious. The boy simply, arrogantly, asks for "his" half of his father's life work's rewards, without having done anything apparently to deserve it—just as God gave us life (and all the riches that entails) with no strings, leaving us free to use it as we will, even against God's wishes. (Think of that next time you meet a panhandler asking for change.)

The boy comes to his senses (as we sometimes do), realizes what a mess he's made of his life, and heads for home, memorizing a set speech to placate his father. But notice the details. The father sees the boy from afar, which shows what? He's been out there every night, peering into the dark, hoping. And the father runs to the boy, not the other way round. He embraces him and kisses him *before* the boy says a word, *before* he apologizes. He doesn't have to *say* anything; all he had to do was come home! And the father *doesn't* say, "I want to know how you spent every shekel of my money before you get back into this house." He doesn't ask for species and number of the boy's sins. He doesn't make him grovel, or feel ashamed, or make restitution. And instead of a penance, he gives him a *party!*

But the older son is even further away from his father than the younger one ever was. The younger boy betrayed his father's love by sinning; the older boy betrayed his father's love by feeling he had somehow *earned* it by his dutifulness. What he forgot was that his father had loved him nine months before he'd seen the boy's face, helplessly, because he was his *son.* He complains of never having received a goat, when his father's given him everything he had left!

The father in this story obviously stands for God, but he stands also, I think, as the model of God Jesus presented us for our imitation. When you say Christians base their lives on Jesus, that's what you mean: We forgive. Before anyone "deserves" it. That's Christianity.

JESUS

How could any one man who lived 2,000 years ago have begun a movement which now numbers nearly two billion people? Think, too, of how many billions upon billions have been Christians since Jesus died. Maybe they've worshiped in different ways; maybe some never worshiped publicly at all, but still signed themselves into hospitals as "Catholic, Lutheran, Methodist." But despite all that, all of them at least claimed Jesus—and Christianity—had the answers to their profoundest problems. No matter how corrupt the Church was at times in our history, no matter what risks were involved in remaining a Christian, no matter how confusing the theological controversies became, all those billions upon billions remained "Christian."

Like Peter, when Jesus challenged his disciples about whether they would leave him when he told them to eat his flesh and drink his blood, all those people said: "Lord, to whom else can we go? You have the words of eternal life: The Answer."

Jesus surely must have been a magnetic man. How else could he have attracted such hardhanded men as Peter and his friends in the boats, shrewd men like Judas and Matthew the tax collector? There is no way Jesus could have looked like the pale, wispy, delicate man we see on so many inexpensive holy cards. In the first place, he was a Jew. He had swarthy skin, and it's hardly likely he'd have had the blue eyes Jesus has in even the best biblical movies. He was a carpenter for 20 years; look at a carpenter's hands. And the message he offered was unnerving: Take up a cross daily, and come follow me; forgive openheartedly. He had to have had some kind of magnetic power to draw such men with such a message— even to martyrdom.

When God decided the Son would become human to show us finally what we were intended to be all along, there were only two choices: male or female. But in the culture they'd prepared for centuries for the Messiah, a woman prophet would have gotten less of a hearing than Jeremiah! Further, perhaps God's choosing a male Messiah rather than a female one is just another instance of God's Trickster taste for unlikely heroes; choosing a male to show God's intentions about acceptance and forgiveness was just one more Cinderella choice, as with stammering Moses and too-young Jeremiah.

Jesus was certainly connected with his "feminine," his Anima. He was gentle, compassionate, inclusive, forgiving even enemies, and for one who had never sinned, he showed an extraordinary empathy for sinners, especially sexual sinners: Magdalene, the adulterous woman, the Samaritan woman at the well. No one ever had to grovel for forgiveness, or give species and number, or do penance; all they had to do was ask. And his message was surely "feminine": love, joy, peace, patience, goodness, mildness. But Jesus' *method* of spreading that message was unrelievedly "masculine." He was not the "Warm Fuzzy" we find in our sugary hymns and church art and biblical movies.

PILGRIM

Jesus' whole public life was a pilgrimage. He was called from the serene security of Nazareth out onto the road for three years. "The fox has his burrow, but the Son of Man has no place to lay his head." And his message calls us to come out on the road, too. Perhaps not literally into a seminary—though that's not out of the question—but at least out of our self-protective cocoons: to make a difference, not just to survive.

Jesus' pilgrimage had an ultimate goal: Jerusalem and Calvary, where he'd be enthroned as King—in a very unpredictable way. At the very end, he was tempted to give it all up, but he went through the door of death freely yielding his spirit to his Father. And came back, from what before that moment we had all thought was the final pilgrimage.

PATRIARCH

Even men older than he treated Jesus like a father. And Jesus obviously loved children, even dirty, snot-nosed brats. (Notice that children in biblical movies all look as if their mothers had scrubbed them for the occasion, unlike the urchins you see in the streets of Israel today.) He "fathered" his disciples, teaching them, correcting, teasing. After Peter's three denials and after the resurrection, Jesus doesn't make Peter crawl; he only asks him, three times, "Peter, do you love me?" And when Peter says that, of course he loves Jesus, that's the end of it.

Jesus seemed especially fatherly to Peter:

Jesus: Who do *you* say I am?

Peter: You are the Christ.

Jesus: Very good. And the Christ must suffer and die.

Peter: Oh, no, no. Never!

Jesus: Get behind me, you satan.

That's tough love. And in Jesus, we see God, the Father.

WARRIOR

Jesus came into enemy-occupied territory, in which "he who is not with me is against me." He was not just a nice moral teacher; you don't crucify nice moral teachers who preach nothing but turning the other cheek and remaining meek and mild. He was a subversive, come to overturn our expectations, to uproot the entrenched belief that we could ransom our own lives simply by keeping our noses clean and observing the Law strictly.

After the temptations in the wilderness which tested the realization he had at his baptism ("If you *are* the Son of God, turn these stones into bread!"), he came into the synagogue and gave the inaugural address of his campaign: "The spirit of the Lord is upon me, because he chose me to bring good news to the poor, liberty to captives, sight for the blind, freedom for the oppressed. I have come to proclaim the amnesty of God." And he said later, "I haven't come to bring you peace; I've come to bring a sword." The demons he challenged knew what Jesus was about. So did the scribes and pharisees; that's why they countercharged that he, not they, were working in the hands of the Enemy; that's why they executed him.

But Jesus didn't use a literal sword. When Peter tried to defend him with one at his arrest, Jesus snapped at him to put it away: "Those who live by the sword die by the sword." Rather, Jesus used stories, exhorting his audience to reach out to their neighbors and make a difference.

In the final battle, it seemed even to his own disciples the Enemy had won and Jesus had lost. But as Jesus had said, "Unless a grain of wheat fall in the earth and die, it remains a single grain. But if it dies, it yields a hundred-fold." And Jesus' death surely has multiplied him.

FRIEND

Jesus was a good friend. He had a special affection (and tolerance) for the bumbling Peter. John's gospel makes a point of describing the youngest disciple as "Jesus' favorite," and of all Jesus' male followers, only he had the courage to stand witness at Jesus' crucifixion.

But Jesus was also obviously openhearted to strangers: the lame, the stammerers, the blind, lepers. Even in the case of the rich young man who felt unable to leave his goods when Jesus invited to become an apostle, the gospel said Jesus "looked on him and loved him." He was a welcome guest with Martha, Mary, and Lazarus, and he wept at Lazarus' tomb. We have it on that best authority there is nothing unmanly about weeping for your friend.

KING

Jesus was the Messiah, a leader, but not in the way many leaders are—world beaters like Hitler, Hugh Hefner, Al Sharpton, who simply discern which way the parade is heading and get in front it, giving people and press what they want. No one can say that of Jesus. His message is assuredly not what we—or the apostles—wanted to hear: If you want the first place, put everybody else's needs ahead of your own; don't worry about what you wear or what you eat but about what's important; it's as easy for a rich man to get into the Kingdom as for a camel to poke through the eye of a needle.

Unlike Solomon, Jesus didn't fall in love with his own power. Nor was he trying to take charge of people's lives, but rather to convince them to take charge of their lives themselves. When asked who was the greatest in the Kingdom, he lifted up a little child. He told his disciples — the first pope and bishops of the Church—*not* to be like civil authorities who lord over others and impose burdens on others they do not carry themselves. Their purpose was to minister—to serve—and in order to show them how a true King acts, he bound a towel around his waist, got down on his knees before them, and washed their feet.

WILDMAN

Jesus was at home in the wild. After Jesus' baptism and call, Mark says the Spirit "hurled" him into the desert. And there he rejected the easy way to conversions, buying faith with bread or miracles or power. Whenever he was weary of the burden he had taken on himself, he went out to the wild to pray, to be with his Father.

Although Jesus' message may be "feminine"—heal, forgive, love—his method was unrelievedly "masculine." It was no domesticated male who strode into the Temple and cleared it with nothing more than a handful of rope and his own towering rage. If you want to disabuse yourself once and for all of any suspicions Jesus was a wimp, read Matthew 23, 39 verses of searing invective against the teachers of the Law. But put it in context; it was the equivalent in his day to standing up to a diocesan priests' council, with the bishop present, saying: "They don't practice what they preach. . . . They wear flamboyant costumes. . . . They love to be fawned on. . . . Hypocrites! . . . Blind guides! . . . Whitewashed tombs! . . . Tangle of snakes!" Imprudent, to say the least. Little wonder they wanted to shut this Wildman up.

HEALER

This needs little consideration here, since it is so obvious Jesus spent his entire public life doing little else but healing: healing people's bodies with his power, healing people's souls with his forgiveness, even trying unsuccessfully to heal the warped souls of the pharisees and scribes, who refused to admit they had any need of healing. We are called to do the same.

But again, realize that Jesus' method of healing was in no way "feminine," bathing the victim's brow, soothing fevered fears. When he confronted illness, physical or psychological, his method was aggressive: "Shut up. Come out of him!" and "Take up your mat and walk."

PROPHET

Again, this is so obvious in Jesus that it needs little discussion here. Jesus was nothing if not an idealist who refused to quit. Had he been pliable, willing to compromise, open to a "deal," he never would have been crucified. It is mindless to attempt to "defend" Jesus as a man of unshakable principles.

TRICKSTER

The Jesus we see in so many biblical movies and hear about in so many homilies seems so unthawably sober and solemn, we get the notion Jesus actually was like that. Just as the movies turn Moses into chesty Charlton Heston (when he was far more like Don Knotts), they turn Jesus into a scarcely human—much less male—personage whose smiles always seem guarded, walking through these dirty people like a concert pianist trapped among stevedores.

But Jesus was actually very playful. He loved kids. He tweaked the hypocritical noses of the "blind guides . . . white-washed tombs . . . tangle of snakes." Surely there's an element of humor when he says of the pharisees, "You're so picky you gag on a gnat in your drink but you'll swallow a camel whole." He teased little Zaccheus, the tax collector, who was so small he had to climb a sycamore tree to get a good look at Jesus passing by. Jesus says nothing of Zaccheus' extortions, only, "Zaccheus, come down. I'm having lunch with you today." And what touching humor Jesus showed in calling a klutz like Peter "Rocky."

Like his Father, Jesus also upends our expectations. "Happy are the poor . . . the first shall be last . . . love your enemies." And he gives one of the best lines in John's gospel to Pilate, the man who condemned him to an unjust death. When Pilate presents the battered, thorn-crowned Jesus to the crowd, he says, "Look! This is your King!"

And truer words were never spoken.

For further discussion see the appendix,
pages 189–190.

10 A RETREAT
FOR MEN OF ALL AGES

Suggestions for using this book in a retreat setting
What follows is merely suggestive. It should, of course, be adapted to persons, places, and times.

Advance Preparation: The team of men conducting the retreat should have read the whole book, and it would probably help if they read at least one of the books on the new men's movement: Robert Bly's *Iron John,* Sam Keen's *Fire in the Belly,* or Patrick Arnold's *Wildmen, Warriors, and Kings,* on which the present text so much depends.

The men should familiarize themselves with the questions on each biblical figure, pick and choose which questions they feel most comfortable posing to the boys, and ready themselves to answer the questions offered here for the boys to ask them after each session. If there are any questions offered for the boys to ask which the team—or even a particular member—would feel uneasy facing, simply delete the question, at least from that particular member's group sheet.

Location: The most likely place would be a retreat house, if the group is relatively large, or a campsite, but a large home would serve. But it would be far better to have the retreat away from the school or parish, preferably near water and woods, which tend to make even the savage breast meditative. As much as possible, the atmosphere should be laid-back and easy, comfortable clothes, informal meals—probably best cooked by a team of boys and men, with other boys and men setting up and cleaning up rather than a staff doing it. The shared work breaks down shyness and barriers.

Duration: The process outlined here envisions beginning on a Friday evening and ending early Sunday afternoon, although it could be done on two or three different Saturdays. [Note: If experience serves, the boys will want to stay up late talking—either among themselves or with the men. That's good, but set a limit so they're not cross-eyed for the morning session. Also, it's ideal to schedule the retreat on a long weekend so that the men and boys can sleep in on Monday. If the retreat is going to work, it's going to be work.]

Accommodations: It's good if fathers and sons share a room or a tent; when the lights go out, there is a lot of good talk that can go on. If a boy is without his own father, it might be better that he bunk with one of his pals and his father or with a couple of other boys and a father who has no sons with him. It's problematic whether to invite unmarried men to be on the retreat team, since there are questions about marriage and fatherhood an unmarried man would be able to answer only notionally rather than from experience; the individual group will have to decide.

No TV, no radios, no Walkman. Essential.

Schedule: What follows is also suggestive. Don't let a pre-set schedule strangle the Spirit. If as the weekend progresses the facilitators think the boys need a question box or a free-for-all or touch football game, so be it. *The most important early goal is establishing trust, and right after that is establishing vulnerability to one another. The content of this book is not Holy Writ. Far more important that it serve as a provocation to thought among the members of the team and the boys themselves. Scrap it all if need be.

One possible format:

Friday
6:00 pm	Arrive, settle in
7:00 pm	Dinner and cleanup
8:00 pm	1. HERO and questions, all together
8:45 pm	One man with two or three boys; perhaps easier fathers with sons for this opener
9:30 pm	A bonfire or singalong or something

Saturday
7:30 am	Rise
8:00 am	Breakfast and cleanup
9:00 am	2. ABRAHAM and questions
9:45 am	One man with two or three boys; not the fathers with their own sons
10:30 am	Break
10:45 am	3. MOSES and questions
11:00 am	One man with two or three boys in different groupings from before
12:15 pm	Break
12:30 pm	Easy lunch and cleanup
1:00 pm	Games, walks, snoozes
2:30 pm	4. JONATHAN and questions 5. SOLOMON and questions [SOLOMON might overlap other archetypes]
3:15 pm	One man with two or three boys in different groupings from before
4:00 pm	Break
4:15 pm	6. ELIJAH and questions
5:00 pm	One man with two or three boys in different groupings from before

5:45 pm	Drinks: alcohol for the men who wish, soda for the boys and those who wish
6:30 pm	Dinner and cleanup
8:00 pm	7. JEREMIAH and questions
8:45 pm	One man with two or three boys in different groupings from before
9:30 pm	Bonfire? "Man for All Seasons"?

Sunday

7:30 am	Rise (if you're able)
8:00 am	Breakfast and cleanup
9:00 am	8. JONAH and questions
9:45 am	One man, probably with his sons and other boys without fathers
10:30 am	Break
10:45 am	9. JESUS and questions
11:30 am	One man, probably with his sons and other boys without fathers
12:15 pm	Break
12:30 pm	Mass, at which the father or "father" gives each of his sons or "sons" a token that will be meaningful and memorable
1:15 pm	Barbecue (See note on p.135)

Ambience: The places where the large and small groups meet should be comfortable—without being "sprawly." Kids love to sprawl, but it loses a great deal of focus. Also, by Saturday afternoon, they'll all be falling asleep on you.

Stories and Questions: If the group is large, the team will have to decide between the advantages of having several men each with his own smaller group or having the camaraderie of the whole group together, then breaking into smaller groups for the boys' questions to the men.

The readings take six or seven minutes; feel free to cut wherever you think useful—or drop a story, or substitute another.

One strategy is to have one of the boys prepare and read the story with the help of one of the adults. They'll probably need some help with the unfamiliar biblical names. It's a good idea to give them the showcase, but there is also the problem of seeming favoritism. Also, although giving the boys a chance to read is good, the more important point is that the story be as effective as it can be. Perhaps in the long run, it's best that the best adults read the stories.

There are eight sessions, so it would be ideal if there were at least eight men as facilitators, one to prepare each story session so that no individual is overburdened.

The questions for the adults to pose to the boys are merely suggestions, a grab bag from which to choose the most agreeable. Nor are they exhaustive; the leader of the particular session might come up with far better. The author has put an asterisk (*) beside questions he believes ought at least to be touched on.

Small groups: The team can merely photocopy the questions from the text and give them to the boys, or they can come up with their own questions—even a question sheet for each individual leader for each story. But the adults should have had a chance to look them over to be prepared for what might come. Nor are the questions limiting, merely something to start the boys off if they happen to be shy. If the weekend has been working, they should be able pretty quickly to come up with questions they honestly find puzzling or more meaningful to them.

Vulnerability: The men on the team have to be ready to be as open and honest *as each one can.* There is no need, for instance, to tell boys, "Well, my wife was pregnant so we had to get married." But it will be perhaps even a soul-saving experience for these boys to know that it's all right for men to be vulnerable to one another, honest about their failings when they trust the people to whom they commend them, that the problems the young men are going through were not invented when they themselves first underwent them. Don't be surprised if a boy—even not your own son— comes up and asks if he can take a walk with you and "go to confession." Judge for yourself whether this confidence really needs the sacramental attention of a priest; quite often it won't. But the adult should offer himself as a confidant in the future—or if that's not possible, ask the boy if he knows some adult male he'd feel confident in sharing his puzzlements with as he's shared with you. Unless you make the boy specify an individual, he's likely never to do it.

Beware of showing any judgmental shock if a boy tells you, in confidence, that he suffers from something for which you personally have an ingrained repugnance; for instance, that he's afraid he might be homosexual. You're the Christian he came to, hoping to find Jesus Christ. But be very sensitive to the fact that you're (most often) not a professional, and try to steer him in that direction. [Along that line, it would be of great value if there were a psychologist or psychiatrist among the school or parish fathers who could be along for the retreat.]

Letters: One very moving experience can arise if the team who runs the retreat can, without the boys' knowing, ask their mothers—and perhaps other members of the family— to write letters to them, telling them what it means to have such a son, what the writer feels about this boy now beginning to take his place in the adult world. Bring the letters along and pick a time when the boy has a chance to go off by himself and read them, perhaps before the final Mass.

The Mass: The priest should choose readings that fit the theme of the weekend: achieving Christian manhood. One set of readings that might be appropriate are: the call of Isaiah (6:1-8), the invitation to happiness (Philippians 4:4-9), and the call of the apostles (Luke 5:1-11).

The symbol each boy receives at the Mass (after or just before Communion) should be both meaningful and memorable. Some retreat groups give a small wooden cross on a rawhide thong; some give a lapel pin. It could be that the fathers who have their own sons with them would rather bring something completely personal to them and give it to their sons at the Mass—although this could, again, be painful for boys whose fathers are not there. The group could even give a copy of this book so that the boy could have something to refresh not only the experience of the retreat but its content—even years later in college or after. It would be good, too, if the Mass could segue uninterruptedly into the barbecue, as the Last Supper did.

The Barbecue: It is the author's hunch that this would be an excellent time for the boys to share a beer with the men, as a kind of rite of passage and as a reminder that alcohol is also part not only of an adult personality but also part of an adult character. But the team—or individual fathers—will have to decide. Whatever the decision, it should be unitive rather than divisive. But one should always remember that Jesus was accused of giving scandal because he enjoyed drinking with his friends. And better to form drinking habits with one's own father than with strangers, especially inexperienced, very young strangers.

1. THE HERO

[Read the story with one boy reading the narrator, one reading Rabbit, and a man reading the farmer.]

Questions After the Rabbit Story:

[The first question after each story should be something like: "Can anybody tell us what the core of the story is, what God was trying to tell the listeners about the kind of men God wants us to be?"]

1. Write "SUCCESS" on a piece of cardboard and ask each of the boys, one by one, to say what that word means to him, concretely, as an individual. Then, ask the men. What similarities between the boys' answers and the men's answers? How did they differ? Can any boy say why they might be so different?

2. Can anybody tell us the difference between a grown-up man and an adult man?

3. Does any of you know of some man you'd call a hero—or at least someone you'd admire *as* a good man, rather than as a sports hero or a big money-maker? What makes him admirable?

*4. What's the difference between image and substance, between "personality" and "character"—as in "He's got lots of personality" as opposed to "He's got a lot of character"? Which is more important, more permanent?

*5. How much do you guys think your idea of an ideal man is influenced (even without your fully realizing) by *Playboy,* the Marlboro Man, Tom Cruise, Eddie Murphy, Marky Mark? How much do face and body have to do with being "manly"? Is there any other meaning to the word "manly"? How would that "show" in a man?

6. Do the heroes in old-time movies or novels seem kind of corny? Naive? Can anybody say why? Are they *really* naive?

*7. Can anybody list the qualities that a good husband ought to have? A good father?

*8. Now that you've passed puberty, what difference do you think those changes in your body—and therefore in your inner self—will have on your relationships with: your parents, your siblings (especially the younger ones), girls, your work in school, your parish? Will the only difference be that you can drive, maybe drink a few beers on the sly, feel horny?

9. Find the poster "L'Enfant" (a "herk" with his shirt off, staring in awe at his baby on his knees). Half the girls in most of the college dorms in the country have that picture on their walls. Why do you think they do?

*10. How much does financial success and security have to do with your idea of a fulfilled man? Do you guess that, say, ten years out of college, you and your family will be living at least as well as you and your parents are living now? What concrete evidence do you have in the way you live and work at school now that would give legitimate basis for that hope?

[It might be good to photocopy and pass out pages of the text which give all the archetypes, their shadows, and what will balance that shadow, but beware of making the weekend too much "like class." Don't belabor it.]

Questions for the Boys to Ask the Men About the Hero:

1. Is this whole process as unnerving to you as it is to most of us? Can you tell us how and why?

2. When you were our age, who were your heroes? They're probably just names to us, but can you tell us something about them and why they were heroes to you?

*3. Who are your heroes now? Could you tell us why?

*4. When you were our age, what did you *hope* to become, sort of in your dreams? Realistically, what did you *expect* to become? Did things turn out differently from what you hoped and expected? What factors changed your dreams and expectations?

5. If you had one decision in your life at around our age that you could change now, what would it be?

6. Did you ever feel like Rabbit, so fed up you wanted to chuck it all and run away? How did you find your way out of it?

*7. Was school ever a drag for you? Do you think there's any real reason for going to school maybe 16 years except just to get a good-paying job? [75% of the men employed in the country did not graduate from college; steelworkers get $30 an hour.]

*8. Was there ever a time when you thought going to church was just a waste of time? Could you tell us why? And could you tell us what changed your mind?

9. How much does what your friends think a real man is affect what you think one is?

10. How much does what women—especially your wife—think a real man is affect what you think a real man is?

---

2. ABRAHAM

Questions After the Abraham Story:

[Can anybody tell us what the core of the story is, what God was trying to tell the listeners about the kind of men God wants us to be?]

1. Can some of you tell us what your expectations are for the rest of this year? For the years till you get to college?

2. A lot of times something looks appealing and yet some "voice" inside you tells you it's not just

dangerous but pretty bad. Where do you think that "voice" comes from?

*3. It must have been pretty upsetting for Abram to leave behind all he'd worked for and start over. Sometimes things that looked unpleasantly scary (like trying out for a team) turned out to be far better than you expected, a real life-giving experience. Has that ever happened to you guys? What does it say about "invitations" that seem at first repellent?

*4. Talk to us about school, because after all, that's your job just as my job is _____. Don't talk about the easy parts like being with your pals and playing sports. Talk about the meat of it: class, homework, tests. Is it all mindless drudgery? Would you say you give your parents an honest day's work for an honest day's pay? If not, why not?

     [The focus on their actual school week is important and should recur throughout the weekend. School is, after all, one-third of their week; it is their work, for which their parents subsidize them to the tune of about $20,000 a year. But they find it difficult to accept that parity. And yet if they don't give an honest day's work for an honest day's pay, that's grand larceny. What's worse, it not only makes their week a drudgery but it also is a horrific waste of their God-given "talents."]

5. We can all be honest here: Do you honestly feel like a somebody or like a nobody, a leader or a follower? We'd all like to *think* we're leaders, but if you do

think that, how does it show concretely in your ordinary week? If not, do you think your inner Pilgrim would be "ready when the lightning struck"? A lot of you guys have been silent on this one; Why?

6. Can you think of just one thing in your school that ought to be changed? What? Why is it important? If it's important, what could you—concretely—do about it?

7. Does the job you do when you finish your schooling make any difference—as long as it pays well? What kind of job would you *like* to do when you get out of college "even if they didn't pay me"? What would keep you from pointing your life toward that job, starting right now?

*8. What *one* quality should a father have to offer his son that no one else could supply, even the mother? Do you think you guys have at least a beginning "hold" on qualities like that? If not, where do they come from?

9. Why was Abraham a failure as father for Ishmael?

10. Can anybody explain what God was doing in asking Abraham to sacrifice Isaac, whom he'd waited for so long for God's promises to come true?

Questions for the Boys to Ask the Men About Abraham:

1. Have you ever had a time when God upset your expectations? Could you tell us about it and how you made sense of it?

*2. Have you ever had a time in your life when you prayed and prayed and God delayed? How did you keep going, trusting God?

3. When you were in school, what was more important: your big successes or your big mistakes? Can you explain that?

*4. When you and your wife really disagree, like Abraham and Sarah, how do you settle it?

*5. Can you tell us what it's like being a father? What are the things you enjoy the most? Fear the most? What are the secrets of "leading" children?

6. What was it like the first time you gave one of your kids the car keys and let him or her go driving alone?

7. When one of your kids is out late on a weekend evening, do either you or your wife stay awake until they're home? If not, can you say why? If so, why? What goes on in your mind?

8. What's the hardest thing you ever had to do as a father? If you had it to do over again now, would you do it at least in some ways differently?

9. What's been your biggest joy as a father? Can you tell us why? What does a man invest in his children besides money?

10. How much are you involved with your immediate neighbors? With your parish? With the schools your

kids go to? Is there some way that what you get out of that involvement could help us understand what it's like to be an adult Christian man?

3. MOSES

Questions After the Moses Story:

[Can anybody tell us what the core of the story is, what God was trying to tell the listeners about the kind of men God wants us to be?]

1. How were the Israelites in Egypt like the slaves in the American south and the Jews in Nazi Germany? They outnumbered their guards; why didn't they rise up and escape? Are there any people in our society who are "enslaved"? What could we—as fellow human beings and Christians—do about them?

2. Can anybody say why the Pharaoh was so unwilling to let the Israelites go? He did nothing but complain about them—their eating, their breeding, their work. Why would he refuse to let them go? Does that give any insights into leaders today?

*3. Are there any people you can think of in our time who are like Pharaoh? Anybody in your school? How do we men deal with the "pharoahs" we encounter in work and at school? Give up?

4. How is Moses like Abraham?

5. Moses is a warrior, and yet unlike any stereotype of a warrior. How is he different from Rambo? How is he like Dr. Martin Luther King, Jr.?

6. Can anybody tell us what a samurai is? Or who Yoda the Jedi knight was? How do they differ from Hell's Angels? What do they have that keeps them from "wilding"?

*7. Who are the Moses-Warriors in our day? What are they fighting against? How?

*8. Can anybody explain: "No one can degrade you without your cooperation"?

*9. In the context of the story, the means Moses used to convince Pharaoh were physical miracles. Now, not too many of us can use that kind of persuasion. What's left to us?

10. Think of just one *concrete* situation in your school that you firmly believe has got to be changed. Now, concretely, what steps could you take to at least begin to have it changed? If at first you failed (as Moses so often did), what would you do?

Questions for the Boys to Ask the Men About Moses:

1. Can you tell us about a time when you yourself were a "warrior," even against a small injustice—when you stood up to be counted, no matter what anybody else said? What did it feel like? When it was over, did you feel changed as a man?

*2. Was there ever a time when you felt like a coward? Or when you were at least afraid of a challenge? Could you help us understand what a man can do when he's afraid?

3. Have you ever *outwitted* a "pharaoh type"? Could you tell us the story?

4. Have you ever learned something from having been too cocky and self-confident? Have you ever felt, "Well, I can do this without any help from anybody," and found you were wrong?

*5. What are the things—maybe even little things—you just refuse to put up with? Why are they important enough that they make you refuse to be an "innocent bystander"?

6. How do you think I should deal with the bullies I meet in school and the neighborhood? Let me tell you a specific case: _____. What do you think I should have done, as a man?

*7. When you're in charge—at work or in your family—and you're asking people to do what you're convinced is right, but they grumble and gripe like Moses' Hebrews, what do you do?

8. When your superiors make a decision you think is not good—or even immoral—what can you do? Do you just have to shut up and go along with it? If it were bad enough, would you really go as far as threatening to quit unless they changed?

9. Can you tell us about a time when you tried and tried to get people to change but—after a long, long time—you finally saw you just couldn't get them to change, at least for now? Do you just have to give up, or do you just have to keep going back, even when you believe the job is impossible?

*10. Nobody gets a "dream child," not even *my* parents! How do you adjust your expectations to the things your kids are honestly capable of? How can I apply that to my expectations of my parents, my brothers and sisters, my teachers, my friends at school? And myself?

---

4. JONATHAN

Questions After the Jonathan Story:

[*Can anybody tell us what the* core *of the story is, what God was trying to tell the listeners about the kind of men God wants us to be?*]

1. Jealousy is a real friendship killer. Initially, it's an emotion that just rises up, without thought. You feel left out, ignored, not valued, and naturally it hurts. But you do have the potential to control it—just as you can control anger. How? Sometimes it comes down to bowing to the truth: He/she loves someone more than me. Like a grudge, jealousy harms others—as Saul's did—but it also harms oneself. At the very least, it's a strong indication of insecurity.

*2. God seems to have the most unlikely favorites: shrimps like David, stammerers like Moses, boys like Jeremiah. Does that pattern in God's preferences say anything to you guys about how you feel about yourselves?

*3. Jonathan had problems with his father. What does a boy do in a case when his father is pretty clearly wrong? Confronting often makes things worse. What recourse does a boy have?

4. What lesson does David teach us in sparing Saul's life? Do you think you could have done that? If not, why?

*5. Love is a strange reality, and often we use the word "love" wrongly. Think of a relationship in which you're absolutely, unquestionably sure it's love. (Hint: mothers.) What kind of qualities does that relationship have, concretely?

6. Tell us how you react personally to: "Set those you love free; if they come back to you, they're yours; if not, they never were." Is that scary? Why?

7. Cliques aren't all bad. They give a man a sense of belonging, a brotherhood one can count on. What makes them bad?

8. Let's try playing the game of Trust and analyze the reactions.

*9. Think of the progress of friendship with just *one* male you trust entirely. Was it worth the risk at each stage? What inside you prevents you from having more very good friends?

10. Do you have a Paul? A Barnabas? A Timothy? If not, what are you missing?

Questions for the Boys to Ask the Men About Jonathan:

1. Have you ever felt betrayed by a friend—especially someone in authority you considered a friend? How did you handle it? Was the friendship more important that the betrayal?

2. Can you share with us a time when your "friends" wanted you to go along with something you instinctively felt was wrong?

3. You have friends who've been your friends longer than we've been alive. What makes them last that long? Do you have to be with them a lot, or are they still important to you even though you hardly ever see them?

4. Shouldn't a man "make it on his own"? Isn't that what *makes* a man, self-reliance?

5. Can you tell us the greatest test of your loyalty to a friend and how you dealt with it?

6. When a friendship becomes a one-way street, and you seem to be doing all the giving, is it still worth working at it?

7. When you pray, do you find it hard to yield to God, to let God have reasons he's unable to share with you?

8. Could you tell us why it so difficult to say "I honestly love him" about another man?

9. What did you do when you honestly thought your father was wrong?

10. Right now, each of you adults are Pauls to us, and we're Timothys to you. Do you have a Barnabas, too? Can you help us understand why having those kinds of friendships is valuable?

5. SOLOMON

Questions After the Solomon Story:

[Can anybody tell us what the core of the story is, what God was trying to tell the listeners about the kind of men God wants us to be?]

*1. We don't have much use for royalty in our country. And yet we do need leaders. Why? Tell us about people who are leaders in your school or your neighborhood. What kinds of qualities do they have that make people willing to follow them?

2. President Harry Truman said that the secret of leadership is to make people do what they don't want to do—and be happy doing it. What does that mean? How do you think a man could develop the skills to do that? What would those skills be?

*3. The story says Solomon regressed from being Solomon the Wise to being Solomon the Magnificent, and that he was "overcome by his own power." Doesn't that seem strange? Doesn't it seem to fly in the face of what we think is really important in life: money, fame, sex, power?

4. This may seem a pretty head-trip question, but what effect does power too often have on wisdom?

*5. Solomon was also defeated because he went over to the false gods of the Canaanites and others. We don't have any literal "idols" today, but what *are* the false gods our society offers to us to "worship"? Who are the "voices" that are offering us those false gods? How influential are they on you guys? On your ideas of what's really important? On your concrete choices?

*6. What good are commercials—on TV, in magazines, on billboards, etc.—for the economy of our country? People say they never really listen to them; they go out and get a snack when they come on. But companies spend megabillions on them every year— surely not because people "never really listen to them." What effect do they have on your values and priorities (like greed)? What effect do they have on your honest freedom to choose what *is* right rather than what "they" *say* is right?

*7. What do you think magazines like *Playboy* and the others are saying human sex is for? What effect do they have on your ideas of what's acceptable about sex—even if you don't read them yourself but hang out with guys who not only read them but accept the "*Playboy* mystique"?

*8. [This one is almost guaranteed to be a hornet's nest!] A big part of boys' lives is dominated by music. No problem with that, and no problem with the *music*, which is pretty much morally neutral: sounds can't really be moral or immoral. But the lyrics have a content, a point of view about life. Now a lot of song lyrics are not only morally neutral but sometimes uplifting. But a great many of them offer a point of view on human sexual relationships that is 180 degrees the other direction from what moral people—not just Christian people—would find acceptable. Can you tell us some groups or lyrics that treat sex as a kind of game or just a pastime? That treat women as merely means to sexual release? That demean human sex into just animal sex? Does that have any effect on how you guys view sex?

**9. In recent years the women's movement has convinced a lot of thinking males that, unless they actualize their "feminine" side (the Anima), they aren't only macho pigs but not really fulfilled as males. Today, husbands and fathers do jobs— cooking, diapering, cleaning—that their own fathers would never have thought of doing; it was "woman's work." How does developing those skills and qualities make better husbands? Better fathers? How many of you guys can cook anything more complicated than a burger? How many of you write poetry? Take dance lessons? Is there something "wrong" with that? If not, where do we get our ideas that there is?

**10. Very honestly, where did you get your understanding of sexual relationships? School? Church? Home? The Locker Room College of Sexual Knowledge?

Questions for the Boys to Ask the Men About Solomon:

1. Tell us about the teachers and bosses you've had who "really knew how to run things." What qualities did they have? How do you think guys our age could start developing those qualities, even in small ways? At school? In the parish?

2. How can guys like us keep trying to be leaders instead of just followers? How do you overcome the fear that guys will reject you if you say, "I'm just not going along with that"? Isn't it more important to belong?

*3. How do we keep money from swallowing up all our other values? In the business world, don't you have to prostitute your values at least sometimes—for the sake of your income and what it can do for your family?

4. How do *you* "protect" yourself from falling into the money-fame-sex-power trip? Everybody keeps telling us we've got to read in order to balance what we hear on the TV, but most adults I know don't read much more than the newspaper or maybe *Newsweek*. Everybody seems to take the line of least resistance: flip on the TV or the stereo or the Walkman. Why should I want to do anything different?

5. I'm puzzled by this whole commercial thing. Okay, it does make people buy things they don't really need. But isn't that essential for the economy, no matter what happens in kids' minds? What are we supposed to do: ban them?

*6. A lot of my friends think the stuff the Church says and teachers and parents say is just old-fashioned. Morality changes from age to age and culture to culture, doesn't it? [Get a good understanding of the difference between *objective* morality, out there in the objective natures of things, and *subjective* morality, our fallible opinions as a society or as individuals about what's human and what's less than human.]

*7. This is a tough question, and you don't have to answer it if it makes you too uncomfortable, but how did you first learn about sex? Your dad? The guys? Books? Were you as confused as I've been? Monday mornings guys are talking about how they "scored" over the weekend. I think they're wrong to use girls that way—and even worse to come in and brag about it, using those girls as just a good story. But every once in awhile I say to myself, "Why are they getting away with it? What harm would it really do anybody if both she and I want it?" The same thing about masturbation: What harm does it do anybody? [The best things I've heard about masturbation are: (1) It's not all that bad; but then again it's not all that great either; does anybody really feel "great" after it? (2) There's nothing that much wrong with it except that it's . . . so goddamned lonely.]

8. Do you really buy all this stuff from the women's movement about men developing their "feminine side"? Doesn't a man have to "prove" himself somehow? Don't girls want guys who are sure of themselves and not "soft"? Take guys who take ballet lessons and play the violin; isn't that kind of "dangerous"?

9. Isn't being honest about your own weaknesses itself a weakness? If a father openly confesses his mistakes, doesn't that make him less trustworthy to his kids? Do you think at least adolescent kids should know about the family's financial situation?

10. If you had to pick just *three* qualities that a man ought to start developing in order some day to be a good father and husband, what would they be?

6. ELIJAH

Questions After the Elijah Story:

[Can anybody tell us what the core *of the story is, what God was trying to tell the listeners about the kind of men God wants us to be?]*

1. Tell us about characters like Crocodile Dundee, Tarzan, Indiana Jones. What qualities do they have that sort of sneer at civilization and all it demands? Do they show a side of manhood that our society has "domesticated"? When the Bible says the lion should lie down with the lamb, why do we automatically assume the lion becomes lamblike? What's wrong with that?

*2. We've got to have rules in order to avoid chaos among people who have to live together. But something in a lot of young men resents that, wants to let the hair grow, not shave, go grungy, and run wild. What's good about that? And what's at least a bit dangerous about that? How does a man balance the need for order with the need to be spontaneous? What keeps the Wildman in a man from going crazy: wilding?

3. What does it mean when Elijah hides in the cave? Or when Jesus shouts, "My God, my God! Why have you abandoned me"? Have you ever had times like that? What brought you out of it? When you see one of your friends "hiding in his cave," what can you do about it?

4. Power itself is indifferent. What makes the difference between using it well and using it badly? Some have power because they're smarter, faster, stronger. Tell us about some people you know who use those powers badly.

5. Whether they are men or women physicians or nurses, doctors use "masculine" healing and nurses use "feminine" healing. Can anybody explain what that means? In order to be good fathers and husbands, men have to do both. Can anybody explain what that means?

*6. Can anybody tell us about a time when he got really hurt that made him a lot more sensitive to other people who've been hurt that way? Why is a "wounded healer" a better hope for people in need than somebody who wants to help but who has never been hurt himself?

*7. In every school, in every year, there are boys you just know were the first kids hit in their grammar school dodgeball games. Think of one; just one; get a picture of him. What qualities does he have that seem to make him a "natural victim"? How do you think he got that way? Use your imagination. Now can you think of any *concrete, specific* ways you could begin to help him feel less "different," more welcome? Think of the kinds of people Jesus was always on the lookout for; how is this boy like those people?

8. Do you know a grown-up who refuses to accept his weakness? Tell us about him.

9. In the story, Jezebel is not exactly your best candidate for Mother of the Year. She even out-machos her husband. Think for a moment of one woman you deal with on a fairly regular basis who at least seems like a "Jezebel." One way to deal with her is by confrontation, which usually not only doesn't work but makes things worse. What are the ways a clever man could soften up a Jezebel, perhaps even help her to become a fully realized woman?

10. A lot of guys see the need to develop the personal qualities and skills to be an adult male rather than just a grown-up male, a child in a man's body. But they say, "I really have to get around to that . . . sometime, maybe in college." Why is that most often wishful thinking? If a boy in high school doesn't begin to develop those qualities and skills now, what realistic grounds are there to hope that he'll develop them in college—or even after he's working and married?

Questions for the Boys to Ask the Men About Elijah:

*1. Can you tell us how you personally balance the ways you have to conform in order to get along and the urge to just "tear off"? Do you really wish you could be more spontaneous? When you get in the business world, do you have to do too much "toeing-the-line"? If so, shouldn't I really try to get in all my "spring break" time between now and the time I have to leave college?

*2. What gives you confidence to follow what you know is right rather than going with the crowd? Can you tell us what part God has in your confidence? Can you tell us how to establish a relationship with God, having somebody you know is "with you" even though everybody else seems to be against you?

3. Could you tell us about some times when you've been wounded that have made you a better healer? A better husband? A better father?

4. Are there particular positions government officials take that you think are genuinely immoral? What alternatives do you have? Do you think it's a waste of time and effort to vote, to write letters to editors and congress members? They just toss them on a slush pile, don't they? Isn't it true that nobody without a lot of money and influence can "do anything about anything"? Isn't it better—or at least less frustrating—just to mind your own business?

*5. If some of us think Mass is really important but that the Mass where we go to church is boring or "out of it" or incapable of getting us fired up as Christians, is there anything realistic we can do about it? Is that just one more place where we have to shut up and grin and bear it?

6. A lot of guys we know really sneer at anybody who still belongs to the Boy Scouts or still serves Mass or runs for student government. They say it's not just prissy but naive. Is there anything you can tell us to make us want to hang in there—no matter how much those guys sneer?

*7. Have you ever had a time when you did what Elijah did: just run away and hide, get drunk, deny all the crap? You're obviously here, so you obviously pulled yourself out of it. How? Can you help us with any hints about how to resist getting bogged down in self-pity?

8. When you're down in the dumps, who's the best person to talk you back into the game? Your wife? A friend? If your son ever came to you and said, "Dad, I really think you ought to . . . ," what would be your reaction?

*9. Do you think, now that I'm at least supposed to be starting to become a man, I could have the courage to help my Mom or Dad when I think they're wrong? Do you have any hints on how to turn those situations from being a mutual hassle to being an honest communication? [There are going to be kids who honestly are right and the parents wrong: alcoholism, divorce, fighting. This could be a great opportunity, but it requires tact.]

10. Could you tell us of a time when you used your power over your kids badly? What did you do to heal that?

7. JEREMIAH

Questions After the Jeremiah Story:

[Can anybody tell us what the core of the story is, what God was trying to tell the listeners about the kind of men God wants us to be?]

1. Through Jeremiah, God says the people have chosen "the way to death." In what ways do you think our society has chosen the way to death? A lot of things that it promises will make us happy really don't: Look at Elvis, Marilyn, Janis, John Belushi, Howard Hughes, who "had it all" and yet anesthetized themselves for years and then killed themselves. But is what they say is "the good life" *still* appealing? Did they kill themselves because they were so *happy*?

[Some of the questions given here are repetitious but useful in one session if not used in another. The team should decide what leader uses which ones.]

*2. Who are the "prophets" in our world today? What kinds of evils are they shouting against? Why do you think they do it, even though—as with Jeremiah— people laugh at them and call them kooks and doomsayers? Do you guys feel that, some day, you would be prophets? What would you have to do to begin?

*3. Think for awhile, and each one of you tell us about a real, undeniable injustice in your school—not something surface like haircuts or clothes rules but something substantial. Now what—realistically— could you and a few others start to do about that? Next week?

*4. Don't say, "I'm too young; I'm just a boy." When puberty happened to you, that option was taken out of your hands. Once you're capable of producing a child, you can no longer claim you're still a child yourself. How has this physical change in you changed your relationships—to everybody, including yourself?

*5. What was the lesson God wanted Jeremiah to learn from the potter? If God is *really* God (and what does that mean?), then have we any right to complain that God throws us back on the wheel and makes a completely different pot out of our potential than the kind of pot we wanted to be? When God "throws you a curve"—makes the kind of world where you can break your arm at the height of your best season, allows your best friend to have some terrible disease, doesn't interfere when your parents divorce—what kind of response does a creature have for his Creator?

*6. Wisdom is to be at peace with the unchangeable. What does that mean? Why is it true? Can you make anything out of "If only's"?

7. Jeremiah says, "Change your ways. Stop taking advantage of alien people who look different from us! Take care of the homeless that lie in your streets! Stop ravaging the land and worshiping money!" Does that remind you of any society you're aware of? Jeremiah is talking for God; that's what "prophet" means: "to speak for another." What does he say to you guys?

8. Like Elijah, Jeremiah is tempted to give up. He even bawls out God in no uncertain terms a couple of times. Is it okay to get honestly, fiercely angry at God? Once you've done that, though, as you would with any friend you feel betrayed your trust, what do you have to do to keep the friendship?

9. Edmund Burke said, "All that's needed for the triumph of evil is that good men be silent." Why is that true?

10. In the time we have left in this session, let's brainstorm *concrete, specific* ways a group of students could enlist even more students in a school to make the environment we share just a little less inhuman. [Cleaning up the litter from a length of expressway with a sign that says, "We did this for you; don't make us do it again!"; Getting hardware store owners to donate paint and getting a crowd to paint over the graffiti, with the same kind of sign; organizing a crew to make sandwiches once a month and walking the streets to give them to homeless people; the parish buying an inner-city house—with the help of all the bankers, lawyers, contractors, do-it-yourselfers *and their kids*—and fixing it up for a family; etc.]

Questions for the Boys to Ask the Men About Jeremiah:

*1. There must have been sometime when God didn't "play fair" with you, betrayed your trust, broke your heart. Could you tell us about it? We all know God doesn't "step in and meddle," but God did create a world where such things can happen. Could you help us understand how you began to understand?

 2. What do you think "tough love" means? Where does a father learn to "draw the line" between being too authoritarian and too lax with his kids?

 3. Could you help us find ways to understand our parents, especially when they seem unfair or too tough? [Wise to remember (unlike kids' convictions) love is *not* a feeling. Love is an act of the will; it takes over when the feelings fail, when the beloved is no longer even *likable*.]

*4. How do you—as a provider, as a husband, as a father, as a Christian—keep from burnout? What helps you keep your spirits up, even when things are looking pretty bleak? Does praying help? When you're down, do you try to keep it from your wife and kids or do you share it openly? Why?

 5. How can I make myself care about others—really, not just in some airy way? How do I care about people who put me down, ignore me, seem not to want my help even though I'm ready to give it, lock me out of their cliques? Does there come a time when you just have to say, "T'hell with what they

think of me"? Is that one of the unchangeables that wisdom is at peace with?

*6. You're a parent. What do parents realistically expect of their sons? How does that change after a boy's gone through puberty and begun to become a man? How do I find a balance between what they want me to do and what I want to do? Is there some way I can find out that what I want to do actually is better in the long run for me than what my parents say is? [Be ready to make the distinction between justifiable expectations (acting like a man and not a child) and unjustifiable expectations ("An undertaker was good enough to put you through college; why can't you be an undertaker, too, and take over this business?")]

7. One of the reasons the people wouldn't listen to Jeremiah was that, if they ever really started to believe what he said, they'd have to change their opinions and their behavior. I feel like that sometimes with my parents and teachers. Do you have any hints on how I could be more honest with myself, give them at least an honest listen?

8. What do I do when I'm telling the truth and my teachers and parents refuse to believe it? [One answer is: Always tell the truth, even when it's going to land you in hot water for awhile. Then when you're telling the truth but it looks doubtful, you'll have a reputation to fall back on.]

9. All this stuff about idealism sounds pretty attractive, out here, away from the ordinary week. But how do I keep it up when I go back to the sneers?

10. Speaking of that, how do you make "the switch" from your ordinary mind-set at work and the husband-father mind-set you have to have at home?

---

8. JONAH

Questions After the Jonah Story:

[Can anybody tell us what the core of the story is, what God was trying to tell the listeners about the kind of men God wants us to be?]

1. Who are the lovable tricksters you can name from stories and comics? People like Hobbes, the Roadrunner, Hawkeye. Name some more. What's their "purpose" in human life? In this story, who tries to be the trickster, but who really is the trickster?

*2. Look at all the heroes we've seen so far. Has any single one of them looked even *remotely* promising at the outset? And to give them credit, did any one of them think he was up to the challenge God was offering them, whether they liked it or not? What does that say to you guys when you're tempted to say, "Hey, I'm nobody; I'm just a kid"?

3. God often tries to talk to us through other people, through unexpected and unpleasant jobs. Can you name a few that have been dumped in your lap that you tried to weasel out of? What was the final outcome? Is there a lesson there?

4. When Jonah thinks he's been used as a patsy, what does he forget? What has his making a fool of himself resulted in? Why does he fall into the sulks? As we've seen, we do have a right to get angry with God, even to bawling God out, but what do we forget about the Creator-creature relationship when we continue to sulk and carry a grudge against God?

5. At the outset of the story, Jonah's the kind of guy who likes to keep his nose clean, mind his own business, and generally avoid the spotlight. Do any of you guys feel that's the best way? Was that the kind of man Jesus was? If not, can a Christian legitimately tell himself that doing no harm is enough?

*6. Right now, as the weekend progresses, each of you probably has an unpleasant itch that says God wants you to become different and to make a difference. There's an awful lot of things that need crusading for, and you surely can't handle them all—or even a few. But until you focus on just *one* thing that you *could* begin changing, you'll never do anything, right? Anybody like to say something he's at least thinking about doing something to improve, even in a small way? It might help the rest of us to hear it.

7. Have you ever in the past made up your mind you were going to change something and it actually *worked*? How did it feel? In cases where you tried and people refused to listen or to change, what was your response? Give up? Find a few others who felt the same and go back and try again?

8. When you start to take yourself too seriously, what do you really need? Who could really jog you out of your doldrums, sulks, t'-hell-with-the-world moods? Would you resent it? Would you rather enjoy your misery than be happy?

9. At the end of the story, Jonah has the hunch that after his job in Nineveh, "his rest wouldn't last very long." Why is that? Is that really all that bad?

10. What is God's biggest "trick" on us? [Being God.]

Questions for the Boys to Ask the Men About Jonah:

1. What do you do when *you* take yourself too seriously? Is there anybody who's a surefire bet to bring you to your senses?

2. Do you ever do anything unpredictable? Why? Does it help? Or do you feel your wife and kids deserve somebody steady, someone relatively unchanging?

*3. Was coming on this retreat something you had to "talk yourself into"? What would have made you hang back? Could you tell us the things that have happened here that help you as a father? As just an ordinary Christian?

4. You asked us this question: Have you ever in the past made up your mind you were going to change something and it actually *worked*? How did it feel? In cases where you tried and people refused to listen or to change, what was your response? Give up? Find a

few others who felt the same and go back and try again? How do you answer that?

5. In your work, what are the parts of the job you'd just like to run away from, like Jonah? How do you keep yourself at them? What motivates you? If you say that, in the end, it's all for your family, that's understandable. But how does that help us when we have no families? [Ooops! Not true, kid!]

6. Have you ever felt God might be whispering in your ear that you might be happier, more fulfilled, doing some job other than the one you do now—like being a forest ranger or a musician or a teacher? Would you be scared? Would it be "impossible" even to think of something like that because of your responsibilities to your family?

7. When you chose a career, did you really *choose* it or sort of "fall into" it? Maybe it's too early for us to start focusing on an all-or-nothing career, but do you think we ought to start narrowing down the options? If you could think of one course we should really concentrate on now, what would it be? If you were hiring someone, what would be the first question you'd ask?

8. How much do money worries get a husband and father "down"? If you were having financial troubles, would you let your wife in on the problems? Would you share them openly with your kids, or would you try to spare them the worry? What do you think are the advantages and disadvantages of each choice?

9. This may be kind of grim, but when you think about dying, when you really wrap your head around the fact that one day it's going to happen to everybody, what effect has that on the way you live your everyday life, your choices, your sense of values?

10. What effect do the women in your life have on the way you view yourself as an adult man—your wife, your daughters, your mother, your co-workers, your women friends? Is what women think of you more important to you than what men think of you?

9. JESUS

*1. In the story, what stipulations does the father demand before he gives the son his money? When the boy comes to his senses and decides to come home, the father spies him "from afar." What does that imply? Who runs to whom? The son has a memorized speech; how much of it can he get out? Does the father demand to know how many shekels his son has spent on what? What does that imply? The father doesn't give the son a penance before he can be forgiven; what does he give the boy instead? The second son has never done anything "wrong"; what *has* the second son done wrong? What does this story tell about the relationship of fathers and sons? What does it tell about the relationship of God and each of us, young or old?

*2. How do you guys picture Jesus physically, his face, his physique, his mannerisms? What is the root source of that picture? Has any of you seen pictures in *The National Geographic* of native Jews and Arabs? What do they look like? What do a carpenter's hands look like? Do the pictures we see of "Jesus" give a true picture of what Jesus really looked like? What effect does our mental *picture* of Jesus have on Jesus' credibility?

3. Each of you tell us, what kind of people did Jesus "hang around" with? Does that tell you anything about Jesus' personality? About the kind of people *God* reaches out to?

*4. Except for a few—Peter, Judas, Matthew, John— we don't know much about the kind of men Jesus freely chose to be his hand-picked disciples. How promising were those men to be the leaders of a worldwide crusade? What does that say about what you and I think our talents are and how they can be used?

5. If you could distill Jesus' message down to just *one* word, what do each of you think that word would be? [The author would opt for "forgiveness."]

6. You've all heard a great many gospel stories. What are the stories which show the *manly* Jesus, the Jesus who wasn't going to take any crap?

7. What are the stories that show that Jesus was not only fully "masculine" but also surprisingly unafraid to show his "feminine" side: inclusive, not demanding full payment of debts, fellow-feeling with sinners— even though Jesus was, by definition, sinless?

8. Jesus worked miracles. Is it inconceivable you could work "miracles"? Like what?

9. Jesus unashamedly loved his father. Do you, unashamedly, tell your father you love him—no matter what his faults?

10. Maybe no need to answer this aloud; just try to answer it in your heart where only you and God can hear: What is Jesus calling you to do, concretely, specifically, next week?

*11. In what ways did Jesus show he fulfilled all the male roles we've seen on this weekend:

—The Pilgrim: ready for challenge and change

—The Patriarch: the loving, responsible father

—The Warrior: crusading against popular feeling

—The King: resolutely in charge and caring

—The Wildman: breaking with expectations

—The Healer: offering whatever he could to the needy

—The Prophet: standing up, unafraid

—The Trickster: upending people's expectations of what is proper.

Questions for the Boys to Ask the Men About Jesus:

1. When you were our age, what did Jesus mean to you? Was he kind of "churchy"? Was he a real, virile man? If your picture of Jesus changed, what made it change?

2. Does the Church seem to you—at one and the same time—too "masculine" in its government and too "feminine" in its working-out at the parish level: liturgies, etc.? Can you explain to me what I mean by asking that question?

3. When you pray, do you pray to Jesus? To the Father? To the Holy Spirit? What kind of image of God is in your head when you pray? Any image at all? Where do you find it easiest to pray—in church, out in the woods, in a quiet room? Are there any words involved, or is it just "being with"? Do you ever pray to try to change God's mind?

4. If Jesus had your job (and this retreat is as much for you as it is for us), how do you think Jesus would do it differently from the way you do it? From most of our co-workers?

*5. If Jesus were a high school student like us, how do you think he'd go about it? Not just getting along with and helping other people, but with the day-to-day grind of class and study? Do you think he'd gripe about anything? If so, would it be that there's too much work, too many deadlines, too high expectations? How do you think Jesus would think about spring break? Girls? Money? Security?

6. How do you think looking at the world and people the way Jesus did changes your idea of how to be a good husband and father? Do you think having a relationship with Jesus makes you more vulnerable, more forgiving, more willing to be used?

7. If Jesus were alive today, at my age, what career do you think he'd go into? Politics? Psychology? Communications? Teaching? The priesthood? The Peace Corps? Business? One of the other professions? Or still be a carpenter?

8. If Jesus were alive today, at my age, what do you think he'd do about parish life?

9. This is the last session. If you had one sentence to say to us, what would it be? Think about it. Don't answer too fast. Would it have been the same sentence you would have "planned" to say before the weekend began?

10. The last question isn't a question. Thank you.

APPENDIX:
FOR ADULT DISCUSSION GROUPS

Soul of a Christian Man could provide provender for discussion for groups of Christian men, of whatever denomination, who are interested in enriching their lives both as Christians and as males. Here are questions that might provoke discussion about each of the chapters. Each man may read the chapter and peruse the questions. Then, in a group discussion, each one should feel free to say, "This is the one question I'd like to kick around." Or even better, "I think I found an interesting angle."

1. THE HERO

- Probably no man can reach 30 without falling at least once into the swamp Rabbit found himself in. Explore some time in your life when you felt every direction seemed like a dead end. How did you cope? Was there anyone to help shake you to your senses? Did you resent their seeming callousness to your miseries? How did you find a way out? When you get less dramatically "down in the dumps" periodically, what— or who—pulls you back to perspective?

- Who were your heroes as a child? How substantial were they? What specific kinds of idealism did they reflect within you then? Have your heroes changed? Disappeared? Is it possible to do better than merely "getting by" if you don't have at least some kind of model? Does having heroes seem just a little bit naive at this point in your life?

- By definition, you cannot achieve a vague goal. And yet, would you say your goals have sort of "gone out of focus," eroded by time and hard knocks into just "keeping going"—paying the bills, holding your nose above water, keeping peace at work and in the family? If someone said to you, "Ten years from today, what would you hope to have achieved—specifically, concretely?" what would you say? Less tangibly, what you hope to change within yourself in those 10 years as a man, as a husband, as a father?

- Reflect on the Richard Wilbur poem about Don Quixote. Do you know men who are merely reactive, waiting for time—or fate, or their spouses, or the boss, or whatever—to make up their minds? Is it possible that you could face life more aggressively than you do now?

- "I'm nobody" becomes a self-fulfilling prophecy. In what ways—at work, at home, in the parish—could you be and act more of a somebody? Do you find the liturgy at church unengaging, too "feminine," too much cherishing and too little challenging? What could you and a group of like-minded men do to change that?

- What were your dreams at 18? How has life skewed them—or fulfilled them beyond your hopes? Do you still find zest in your wife, your family, your job? If not, what would put it back? Could you reach out more—coach Little League, work in the community theater?

2. *Pilgrim / Patriarch*

- Abram had his life more or less settled, in order, predictable. In what ways is your life too humdrum, comfortable, domesticated? Is there one thing you'd really like to do, but you keep telling yourself it's too crazy, too non-work/family oriented, too self-indulgent? Something like learning to paint pictures, do carpentry, read more? In what ways do you feel an unnerving challenge from God to change?

- Although no one need share it with the group unless he feels comfortable doing it, be honest with yourself: Which principle most governs your life and choices, the life wish that craves challenge or the death wish that craves being unbothered? What concrete evidence in your week shows that your inner pilgrim is still alive and reaching?

- "Patriarch" is a touchy term in today's Church. On the one extreme, it resonates of paternalism and excessive control, yet on the other it also suggests the Good Shepherd who is always vigilant for his sheep. Toward which of those extremes do you find yourself leaning—as a husband, father, manager of other people? Even if you don't feel like sharing that, ponder for yourself whether you have to soften up or toughen up a bit.

- Talk about a time when God really tested your trusts as he did Abram's, a time when God—or at least the powers-that-be in your life—played unfair for far too long. What sustained you through that arid stretch of your life? Do you find time in your week to take God for a walk and try to achieve some peace and perspective in God's presence?

- What was the closest thing in your life to the moment God asked Abraham to give up Isaac? Losing a loved one, a job, a promotion? Could you help the rest of us by sharing with us what allowed you to hang on, soldier through it?

- Try to isolate just one quality that children would look for in a father that they wouldn't expect as much of in their mother.

3. WARRIOR / MAGICIAN

- Like so many of the heroes God chose, Moses was a very unpromising candidate for such an intimidating mission—a stammerer who was woefully deficient in confidence, who tries for an embarrassingly long time to weasel out of his assignment. Men often (especially in a church context) can feel as negligible as women who rightly complain about being. "I'm nobody—or at least 'they' seem to treat me as nobody." How could we, as a group of intelligent males, make our presence in our parishes more meaningful, beyond reading, ushering, helping with Communion?

- How unrealistic is this idea? We as a group could solicit others of our parish(es), male and female to buy a rundown house in a poor neighborhood—engage the expertise of bankers, lawyers, construction owners and workers, engineers, and refurbish it for a family who could never hope to have such a home. Parishioners who sell fabrics could donate cloth for curtains, furniture store owners could donate beds and chairs, paint store owners could offer paint and brushes. Even the kids could help. Beyond what it would do for that family, what would it do for us as a parish? How unrealistic is that idea? Think of the earliest Christian churches.

- We all have made commitments—to family, to work, perhaps also to the neighborhood and to the parish. And most likely every one of us has come to a sticking point where those commitments become more than ordinarily burdensome, irksome, constricting. Can we each share how we cope, how we do more than merely "hold on," how we maintain peace of soul?

- Picture a group of babies on a blanket—sweet, wide-eyed, exploring. Now picture the same number of adults in a subway car—slack-faced, dull-eyed, enclosed. What got lost? Curiosity, among other things. Imagination, wonder, the quest for the Grail. Let's each ponder where we've lost the zest in living, then share ways we might all get some of that back.

---

4. FRIEND

- Mull over in your minds the two or three or four most special friends of your boyhood.

Remember the adventures you shared. No rush. Savor their faces and your memories of them. Then move on to the closest friends of your youth, in high school and college. Consider slowly how each one, in his own unique way, enriched your life. Then think of your closest friends today, the men you could likely tell things you'd hardly want to admit to yourself. If there are, in fact, few or no men in your present life with whom you share as deeply as you did in your childhood and young adulthood, what concrete means could you take to rectify that impoverishment?

- Having reflected on the male friends of your life, can we pool our ideas of what genuine friendship requires—vulnerability, availability, trust? We all use the word "friendship," but what does it really mean?

- How do your friendships with men differ from your friendships with women?

- Does each of you have a Paul friend, a Barnabas friend, a Timothy friend?

- At one time, your very best friend was a stranger, anonymous, out there in the unfocused wash of faces. What was the first thing that had to happen to let that someone begin the slow progress toward your innermost heart? Not being introduced or talking, but *noticing*. Without that, nothing. Then the person becomes an acquaintance; some few of those become friends—not necessarily bosom buddies, but people you wouldn't mind sitting down with for lunch on occasion. Even fewer became your close pals, because most often you've sacrificed together. Finally, there are the very best friends to whom you could unburden anything without fear of it jeopardizing our friendship. But focus on that first essential step: noticing. Is it possible that each of us walks through our days with blinders on, carefully focused on where we are going and ignoring so many potential friends?

- Why do so many otherwise confident men find the greeting of peace before Communion at best unpleasant?

---

5. KING

- H.L. Mencken said that whoever coined the term "near-beer" was a very poor judge of distance. I suspect the same is true of those who try to smear out the very real differences (perhaps from nature but surely from nurture) between the ways males and females look at life, relationships, values. In what ways do most males look at responsibility differently from most females? Some men take responsibility as seriously (and often as humorlessly) as Marine drill sergeants. In what ways can they learn from women how to temper control with compassion?

- Every one of us has had to deal with petty tyrants such as low-level managers who feel inordinately empowered because they have a clipboard and a set of keys. How many of us dare to challenge them: "Do you realize you're dealing with human beings here?" More seriously, each of us has also had to deal with tyrants who are—like it or not—heavily armed. Can we pool ideas on how we cope with men and women who have very real power over us and who are often in error but never in doubt?

- Even some of the best scripture translations render the Greek word *hubris* as "pride," as in "pride goes before the fall." Absolutely wrong. By *hubris* a Greek meant not genuine pride in a job well done or a life lived as well as one is able to, but rather arrogance, narcissism, self-absorption. However, as a result of what seems like a mere semantic nicety, men and women for generations have shunned a life-giving sense of pride from fear of overweening vanity. Well intentioned but ill-prepared preachers use the same tactic on the gospel injunction to consider ourselves "unprofitable servants." One has to take that injunction as coming from the same Jesus who also enjoined us not to hide our lights under bushel baskets, to shine like a city set on a hill, to climb up on the housetops and be heard. What does that say to each of us?

6. WILDMAN / HEALER

- Our society—and surely our Church—is really more comfortable with domesticated men, sanitized, deodorized, and predictable. But a great deal of vitality drains from our endeavors, whether secular or sacred, when either the workers or the worshipers are uptight, guarded, restrained. To be sure, many of us have been trained to be rather reserved, but "reserved" means one is holding something back, guarding one's security, fearing the cost. How does that attitude, which many men (and women) have, stand up in the face of a crucifix?

- Many of us find liturgies quite uninvigorating, hardly rousing in us a sense of challenge, dotted with hymns most of which sound like lullabies. Let's allow our imaginations to run a bit wild and brainstorm what we, as a group of concerned Christian males, could suggest to those who control our liturgies to make them more engaging to men (and women). How do we preserve the dignity of worship yet rouse Christians to enthusiastic declaration of their faith? Realistically, how can we make worship not only cherishing but challenging?

- Most of the week we spend dutifully, caring for customers and clients, deferring to superiors, shepherding a family, mediating disputes, meting out punishments. There are at least some times to socialize and relax with other people. But each of us needs some time at least once a week to pull out of the crowd and repair our souls. Otherwise, we deal with people at home and at work at times on sheer nerves, like an engine out of fuel and running only on fumes. Can we share ways to remind ourselves that refreshing our spirits is important not only to those we serve but to our stewarship of our own souls? Perhaps more important, can we share ways we've found helpful to make us carve out that re-energizing time from a cluttered week?

- For both males and females, there are two kinds of healing: the "masculine" way of challenging illness, the "feminine" way of easing patients' pain. Very few of us are literally physicians, but each of us faces situations week in and week out where things are out of kilter—an employee who's uncooperative or distracted or too dependent on alcohol, a child who's getting into trouble or dogging it in school, a friend who's devastated by a loss and unable to begin building a life again. How does each of us handle situations like that in such a way that the one suffering not only feels the challenge to change but the conviction that he or she is not alone in the struggle—important, cared for?

7. PROPHET

- Write a page about something that makes you really angry on the local scene, then consider mailing it in to the daily newspaper. You might groan, as my students do, "What good would it do?" But, as it's been said, all that's needed for the triumph of evil is that good men be silent. If we hope not only to be men of honor but Christians, what are the things we as a group ought not to be silent about —at work, in the community, in the local parish and in the universal Church, in our children's schools? Once we've listed them, what then?

- Ponder God's lesson to Jeremiah in sending him to watch the potter. It is arguably *the* most difficult lesson any believer has to learn: To let God be God, to yield center stage to Someone who truly belongs there. It is the unsettling lesson God asked of Job, of Abraham, of Moses, of Jesus. Unless we spend some time along with God, as receptive as Our Lady at the Annunciation, how can we cope with the truth that God is not answerable to us?

- Conversely, many Christians might have learned that lesson of surrender to Good even too well, yielding as helplessly as slaves or dumb beasts of burden, plodding on in dull resignation. But God didn't intend us to be sheep; that's why God gave us minds that bristle in the face of the irrational. Many of us need not only to yield grudgingly to God but to make peace with God. Can we share times like that, when we confronted God with honest anger—then forgave him?

- Like the North Star, an ideal is a guide, not a destination. Without ideals, a man is merely a sheep, a victim of others' choices. But ideals carry with them the burden of confronting others who aren't troubled by them, people content to cocoon themselves from the truth, preferring the security of being unbothered to the challenge of living fuller lives. What keeps us going, even when the rewards are neither frequent nor tangible?

8. TRICKSTER

- We've heard passages from the gospel so often they've lost their capacity to shock. But consider Jesus' call of the apostles (Matthew 4:18, Mark 1:16, Luke 5:1). Jesus drops by their fishing skiffs, tells them to come after him because he'll make them "fishers of men," and—according to the gospels, at least—they "immediately" dropped everything and followed him. On the one hand, that does argue that

Jesus was a far more charismatic and virile man than he often appears in our treacly holy pictures; he had to be pretty overpowering to convince such hard-handed, practical men to follow him on such a quixotic quest. But on the other hand, something skeptical in me balks at that "immediately." That part of me has to suspect the Twelve had to have responded in the same leery way Jonah did to the same kind of request. Nonetheless, Jesus did make the offer and they did respond—and thereby changed the history of the world. Now, would any of us care to share his uneasiness about any voices he might be hearing, whispering unwelcome invitations about "converting Nineveh"?

- Who are the people who keep you sane, and how do they manage to do it? Can we share a few lessons on how to keep those around us from taking themselves too seriously?

- Beyond doubt, there's a humorless grump where you work. Let's brainstorm a list of videos (Marx Brothers, Laurel and Hardy, Tom and Jerry) he or she really "needs." Now, where's the birthday list?

- "Eucharist" means thanksgiving, an act of gratitude. Let each one of us take a few minutes alone with a piece of paper and list, one by one, pondering each face slowly, the people we love—people we might never have met. Then to focus it more tightly and meaningfully, narrow

down the list to the five absolutely most
precious. If you care to, share their names with
us. No one need say why they are so precious,
but they can if they choose. That sharing may
prove to each of us how sublimely gifted we are.

———◆———

9. JESUS

- Like the father in the story, when God decided
  to evolve a species that would enjoy both intel-
  ligence and freedom, God freely set a limit on
  his own omnipotence. He couldn't grant us
  freedom, then allow us to used that freedom
  only in ways he would approve, nor could he
  step in and rectify the situation when we
  misused our freedom. If genuine love required
  the freedom *not* to love, God apparently though
  love worth the risk. Made in the image of that
  same God, each of us does love all kinds of
  people, from the intensity of marriage and
  family outward in ever-wider circles to the less
  intense (but no less real) love of those suffering
  all over the world. But focus only on those we
  hold closest to our hears. In what ways is it
  possible that we might crimp their freedom?
  Sometimes, for instance, from the best of
  motives—to shield them from harm—we might
  inhibit the chance that they learn from their
  mistakes.

- In what ways have the physical depictions of Jesus in Church art and biblical movies warped our sense not only about what this Jewish carpenter actually must have looked like but more importantly diluted the vigor of his message to us? What are the elements in the life of Jesus as we find it in the gospels which contradict the idea that Jesus was *only* meek and mild?

- Like life itself, the person, the actions, the message of Jesus are rife with paradoxes intended to upend our expectations, to wrench our certitudes into another direction entirely from "the conventional wisdom." Let's brain-storm a list of them, starting with the King of the Jews crowned with thorns and enthroned on a gibbet. "If you want the first place, take the last place." Jesus, the Master, on the night before he died, knelt down and washed his disciples' feet. There are more. Far more.

- Ponder awhile and then if you care to share with the rest of us: What does the person of Jesus Christ mean to you, not just as a Christian, but as a Christian *male*?